ALSO BY ALEC WILKINSON

Midnights

Moonshine

Big Sugar

The Riverkeeper

A Violent Act

A
VIOLENT
ACT

ALEC WILKINSON

ALFRED A. KNOPF
NEW YORK
1993

THIS IS A BORZOI BOOK
PUBLISHED BY ALFRED A. KNOPF, INC.

Copyright © 1992 by Alec Wilkinson

All rights reserved under International and Pan-American
Copyright Conventions. Published in the United States by Alfred
A. Knopf, Inc., New York, and simultaneously in Canada by
Random House of Canada Limited, Toronto. Distributed by
Random House, Inc., New York.

Portions of this work originally appeared in *The New Yorker*.

Library of Congress Cataloging-in-Publication Data
Wilkinson, Alec.
A violent act / Alec Wilkinson. — 1st ed.
p.   cm.
ISBN 0-679-41507-6
1. Jackson, Mike Wayne. 2. Gahl, Tom, d. 1986. 3. Fugitives
from justice—Indiana—Indianapolis—Biography. 4. Murderers
—Indiana—Indianapolis—Biography. 5. Murder victims—
Indiana—Biography. 6. Police wives—Indiana—Biography.
7. Police murders—Indiana—Indianapolis—Case studies.
8. Murder—Indiana—Indianapolis—Case studies. I. Title.
HV6248.J215W55   1992
364.1′523′0977252—dc20   92-20382
                                                                                  CIP

Manufactured in the United States of America

First Edition

For
Sara Barrett
and
Frederica Wessler

In the beginning life was good to me.
It held me warmly, it gave me heart.
Of course it does that to all the young,
But back then how could I know?

—RAINER MARIA RILKE
"The Song of the Widow"

CONTENTS

A Violent Act

RAMPAGE

ON THE DAY that began the most desperate phase of his
anxious life, Mike Wayne Jackson rose early—a habit he
acquired in prison. He was forty years old. He lived without
running water, electric light, or cooking gas in a house in
Indianapolis that had stood empty for years before he moved
himself into it one month earlier. He slept on straw in an
upstairs room, or in the back of his pickup truck parked in
the yard. He did not bathe. He told people he knew and
the men and women who were his neighbors that he was
restoring the house, but no one could see that he had made
any progress beyond pulling some weeds in the yard and
nailing plywood over a couple of windows which had no
glass. He was perhaps six feet tall and weighed about two
hundred pounds. He often wore farmer's overalls. He had
a small paunch. His shoulders tended to stoop. He had long
black hair with strands of gray in it, and a long black beard
that covered nearly all of his face. There was some question

of his sanity. On the morning of this particular day—Monday, September 22, 1986—he killed his probation officer with a shotgun when the officer came to the door of his house. In fleeing, he committed other violent crimes in Indiana and Missouri. By the end of the day, he was the most sought-after criminal at large in America.

Nancy Gahl, the wife of the probation officer, recalls that on the morning he died, her husband said, "I wish I had something more exciting to look forward to." Nancy asked what he meant, and he said that he had to go and see "Crazy Mike Jackson," a new client. Mike had been released from prison five months earlier. He spent most of the year he served for a firearms violation taking psychological tests and being asked how he felt, because he was incorrigibly violent and no one could really tell why. His probation was supervised by an officer accustomed to criminals whose cases involved weapons or drugs, or who were prone to behave without restraint, but the officer had lately taken on too much work and by agreement transferred responsibility for Jackson to Tom Gahl. Before doing so, the officer decided that a sample of Jackson's urine should be collected and tested for drugs, and this was the errand that brought Tom to the door of Mike's house.

The people Tom saw tended mainly to be lawyers or accountants who got into trouble over taxes, or people who stole money from the companies they worked for. He was more inclined to counsel his clients than insist that they do what he told them. Often they wrote to thank him for helping get them back on their feet. Often he saw them for appointments at their homes. Gahl had briefly met Jackson the week before, in his office. What Tom made of him is not known, but another man who passed Mike outside

Tom's door recalls being taken aback by the wild look in his eye, his scruffy, dishevelled appearance, and the feeling of menace that emanated from him. For the weekend, Tom brought home a file on Mike, which amounted to nearly a thousand pages of prison and hospital records, doctors' reports, and documents from various courts, but Nancy remembers that he did not have time to read it. Saturday, he ran errands, and Sunday he went to church with his family, took Nancy to a football game and then spent the evening playing a board game with Nancy and their two little boys, Christopher, eight, and Nicholas, four. If he thought about Mike in the meantime, he did not mention it to Nancy. This was the first occasion on which she heard his name. If Jackson was dangerous, she asked, couldn't he come by the office instead, and Tom said, "Please don't worry, things will be all right." A strain in his manner made her wonder whether he wasn't more concerned than he was saying.

Before breakfast Tom went for a run through the streets of his neighborhood. He showered, then came into the bedroom. Christopher, passing the doorway, saw him sitting in front of a turning fan. Tom often told Nancy he loved her and the boys too much ever to be a hero. He also often said he had never heard of a colleague being harmed. She knew that to visit a client he considered a threat he took along a marshal, and that he had no plans to do so on this occasion. When she mentioned once more how she felt, as he left, he said, "I'll stop at the house, and if he's not there I'll leave a card and ask him to come by the office." Then he said, "I wish you wouldn't worry so much." During the fifty-nine years since the program of federal probation began, no officer had ever been killed by a client.

Christopher and Nicholas were in the habit of waving

goodbye to their father as his car left the driveway. Getting ready for school, Christopher had been engaged by his appearance in the mirror of the upstairs bathroom. By the time he got to the garage, his father's car was already turning the corner onto the street.

According to Nancy's reckoning, Tom left the house at a quarter to eight. By five minutes after, he had been shot, had begged for his life and called out to God, been shot twice more, and lay dead on the sidewalk. Nancy had no premonition of his end. Going about the errands of her morning, she never heard his voice in her mind, or saw a vision of his being in danger. Christopher left for school. It unsettles him to reflect that as he sat on the school bus, talking to his friends, his father, whom he loved, was already dead.

EARLY THAT MORNING, Mike went to work with a hammer on a dent to the tailgate of his pickup truck. The sound woke a woman who lived next door. It went on long enough that she got up and looked out the window and saw him. She tried to fall back asleep. How much time passed she is not sure, but she recalls that next she was aware that the sound of hammer against metal had stopped and in its place she heard someone knocking on the frame of Mike's door. She had never known Mike to have visitors. She was surprised he wasn't answering, because she thought he was home; his truck was still parked in the yard. She stepped out on her porch to see who was knocking and saw the profile of a man about five foot eleven, trim, with brown hair and glasses, and wearing a light-blue, short-sleeved shirt and dark blue pants: Tom Gahl. She had no idea who he was, but the fact of anyone's coming to see Mike was sufficient to hold her attention. Tom stood in front of the open door. There was no sound from the house. He knocked again. A boy on a bicycle passed on his way to school. A dog barked. Tom walked back to his car and sat inside briefly, with the door open, then started again toward the house, perhaps intending to leave a note. He had crossed half the yard when Mike charged from the door with a shotgun. Tom turned to run and the first shot hit him in the back of his left arm, below the shoulder, and broke his elbow. The force of it spun him around to face Mike.

A woman who lived in a house on the other side of Mike's heard the shot and thought it was a car backfiring. Or perhaps, she thought, someone had blown a tire. She stepped out her door and saw Mike backing Tom Gahl up at the point of his shotgun; she thought it was her husband.

They had reached the street: Tom had his back to her, and they were coming up the sidewalk toward her. Tom held his left arm to his side. He was bleeding from his wound and the blood was seeping into his shirt. He held his other hand toward Jackson, and he said, "Please don't shoot, don't shoot me, it's not going to do you any good." Jackson advanced. Tom turned his head to one side and said, "Oh, God," and Jackson fired again. The blast struck Tom in the side of his head and knocked him to his knees and then to the ground. The woman did not hear him speak again. A man driving his son to school skidded his car to a stop not far from where Tom lay, and he and the boy watched Mike place the butt of the shotgun against his shoulder and lean over so that the barrel nearly touched the side of Tom's head and pull the trigger once more. Under the impact of the blast Tom's body rose, then fell back to rest, so that he lay with his wounds to the ground, his eyes open and one cheek pressed against the gravel by the side of the road.

Jackson turned and looked at the woman who was standing in the frame of her doorway. There was blood on his clothes. The expression on his face struck her as absolutely empty of any emotion or feeling or spark of life. She thought it looked dead, and so unlike Jackson that she hardly recognized him. He watched her as if waiting to see what she would do, and then he walked briskly back to his house, turning to look at her a time or two over his shoulder. When he got to his porch he faced her and went sideways up the stairs, his eyes never leaving hers. He came out wearing different clothes, and climbed aboard his truck and backed into the traffic on the street and took off. The woman ran to what she believed was the body of her husband. Tom's proportions and coloring were similar to his, at least from the back, and he had left the house an hour earlier wearing the uniform of his job—a light-blue short-sleeved shirt and dark blue pants. Mike woke him that morning with his banging on the tailgate, and he left for work angry enough that she thought he'd come back and got into an argument.

MIKE DROVE about three miles, through a neighborhood of frame and brick houses more or less like those of his neighbors. He drove no faster than the cars around him. He stopped at the stop signs he came to. He drove underneath a highway bridge and pulled to the side of the road. He aimed a can of silver spray paint toward his face and sprayed his beard and his face and his hair. Then he drove his truck into the parking lot of a machine shop and got out. He watched a teenage boy at the door of the shop unloading soda from the trunk of his car. When the boy saw Jackson walking toward him with the shotgun, he dropped the case he was carrying and ran into the shop, passing a man working at a table by the door. Mike leaned into the car to see if the boy had left the keys in the ignition, but he hadn't. As he came around the car toward the door of the shop he passed a window of the office. A woman saw him and yelled, "He's got a gun," and then she ran. The man at the table thought she meant someone was shooting rats in the parking lot with a pellet gun. Mike walked through the door and came up to the table where he stood working.

"I saw the gun," the man says, "and I knew there was nothing I could do, because it was just a big open room behind me—there was no place to run—and he was so close that if he raised that gun up it would have brushed me. It had the barrel sawed off a little so you could carry it under your coat, and he stood there with it for about a minute and a half. His face was all silver and his expression was totally flat—there was just nothing there to it. He didn't seem nervous. I just stood real still and didn't move my arms or nothing, so as not to upset him. He looked me once up and down, checking to see if I was a threat or anything, and then he was staring over my shoulder into the room behind me, looking for the kid, I guess, to get the keys to the car.

"There's an office about ten feet away, with a window looking into the shop, and somebody was in it, staring right at him, and when he saw that, that somebody was watching him and maybe calling the police, I guess, he spun around real fast and ran back across the street to his truck and took off. Except for that he'd been standing real still."

Mike drove in the direction he'd come, until he arrived at a small, boss-and-a-helper market. Parked on the sidewalk outside the market was a step-van belonging to a man delivering bread. Behind the counter was the owner, a man named James B. Hall; the place was called the J. B. Market. Hall hadn't expected to be at the market that day, but a woman who worked for him was sick. A man from a scrap-iron yard across the street was in the market buying coffee.

"I was standing right up beside the wall," this man says, "where they have the machine for those slushy drinks, and he come in the door. I thought he looked like a bum, 'cause we'd had two or three in there, kind that goes along with a shopping cart picking up aluminum cans. He was wearing this long blue coat like a trenchcoat, blue or black, dark color anyway. He walked right past me to the end of the aisle, far as he could go, almost touched me, then he turned around and walked down the other aisle, and the first thing he said was where was the driver of that bread truck. And that's when he brought the gun out. He had his hand through a slit in his pocket to the inside of his coat and he'd been holding it there, down along his leg. He grabbed the barrel with one hand and took his other hand out of his pocket for the trigger. After that I hardly looked at his face. I just kept watching the end of the gun. He walked past me again and asked where the man driving the bread truck was at. Seemed like I saw some kind of paint in his beard, but I didn't look too close. He held the gun at his hip and pointed it at the man behind the counter at the cash register—there's a little aisle there to where the man was standing at the register—and said, 'I want all your money.' It seemed like Jackson just couldn't stand still. He kept pacing and rocking back and forth. I didn't know what he was going to do; I just figured he'd rob the store and be gone, you know, wouldn't hurt anyone. The man started to get the money for him, but it seemed like he was going slow. Jackson said, 'Hurry up,' and the man said, 'I'm hurrying.' He told him a couple more times to hurry up and the man said, 'Okay, okay,' and that's when the gun went off. It was like you fire a rifle in an empty room, it was so loud. It just left your ears ringing. You couldn't tell for sure if he meant to shoot him, or if it was just nerves, but I believe the man might have tried to trip the alarm—he had a little button there by the register—and Jackson may have seen him make a move for that. He was about six or eight feet away when he pulled the trigger and that shot just knocked that man over like you hit him with a door to a safe, into the toothpaste and the cigarettes and the mouthwash, and he slumped down in a kind of sitting position on his side.

"Once the gun went off, Jackson didn't take none of the money. He just said to the bread truck man, 'Okay, buddy, let's go.' The man didn't move right away, and Jackson took a step in his direction and told him, 'I said, "Let's go," ' and they left. The bread truck was pulled right up to the curb so you could just walk from the cab right straight in the door. Jackson backed out the door and across the sidewalk and right into the bread truck. That was lucky for him, because I had a .357 magnum on me at the time and I was just waiting for him to turn his back. It was lucky for me that my coat was covering it, though, because he walked right past me, almost touched against me, and if he'd got a look at it, I would have been gone.

"I seen him drive away in the van, and then I walked behind the counter, and picked up the receiver on the phone with my fingertips because there was blood on it, and I called the police and said, 'There's a man here shot,' and they said, 'Well, what's his condition?' and I said, 'He's dead.' Didn't even have to check his pulse. There was a big hole tore in the side of his head, and he's sitting in a puddle of his own blood.

"I didn't get nervous while the thing was going on, but once he left I was really shook up. I just kept pacing around. The owner had made a fresh pot of coffee and just about the time he got shot it was ready. The police wouldn't let me leave the store. I said to one of those cops, 'Would it be all right if I had some of that coffee?' and he said, 'Okay,' and I drank the whole pot."

The bread truck man: "That shot just exploded in that little store. I was over loading the racks and making my own noise, so I didn't really know of anything going on till I hear that *boom!* Then I straightened up to see what happened.

"He just called me over and we went out. I never even really looked at Jim Hall. I'd known him fifteen years. He was a real nice man, quiet. He'd talk to you if you were talking to him, but mainly he was quiet. He'd made a real go of that store and people around there really appreciated it. He lived by himself and he used to bring his cat to work sometimes and he'd started a retirement plan for his employees, but now he was gone. I just went out the door.

"Once we got in the truck the man stood in the well there

and held that gun across his arm and pointed it right at me. He was real calm. I saw the silver paint. His beard nearly covered up all of his face, and that's where he'd sprayed most of the paint, it seemed like to try to make himself seem older, I guess, like a disguise. He said he wanted to go to the airport and he told me not to break any speed limits getting there. I just did what he told me. It never occurred to me not to. I'd been in the Second World War and I long ago learned that when a guy's got a gun on you, you do what he tells you. He asked if I had any money and I said I had what I'd picked up so far that morning on my route, and I went into my pockets to get it and he said, 'I don't want your money.'

"The trip to the airport is only about five miles from the J. B. store, but it took a while because he got turned around getting on the expressway—he was giving me directions. I had a thermos of coffee on the dashboard, and he took it and drank the whole thing. Meanwhile, he was telling me where to go and he got on the wrong road, and I didn't tell him. We got to the airport, only it was the business end, where they don't have no flights. He saw this guy coming out of a building and walking towards a little kind of pickup truck and he had me pull the van right up behind the man, and he said, 'Now don't do anything crazy,' and then he got out and walked up to the man and put the gun on him and made him give up the keys, and he was gone. I went around the back side of the building and then just shook for about five minutes."

THE CAR that Mike Jackson stole from the man in the parking lot was not a pickup but a jeep. He left the airport.

Somewhere he stopped and bent part of the rear license plate back on itself, to conceal the number. He drove through neighborhoods on the outskirts of the city. He brought the jeep to a stop in front of a house where a young woman was unloading her car.

"I had just taken my husband to work," she says. "One of our cars broke down, and I stopped at a repair place on the way home and they said they'd come by the house and pick it up. So I went home and I was in my driveway, I put my purse on top of the car and I was getting the rest of my things out, and Jackson drove up. I guess he ran out of gas right in front of my house, and he had this shotgun with him, and I saw him walking towards me, and my mind wasn't really working like you'd expect, I just thought he was coming to ask directions or something, I didn't really know what he would want, the sight of it was just so strange, and he asked for the keys to my car, and I started to say they were up there—meaning on the roof in my purse. He put his hand on my arm and told me to get in the car. He asked if anyone was in the house and I said no, because my sister-in-law and my daughter were up there. My daughter came out on the porch then and was saying, 'Mommy, Mommy,' but I didn't acknowledge her, because I was afraid she'd come running across the lawn. As we pulled out the driveway, the wrecker was just driving up.

"Jackson drove here and there and around and I didn't know where he was going. He seemed like he knew where he was, though. All the time, he had the shotgun across his lap pointing right at me. He asked if I had any money and I was looking through my purse and all I had was some change because I hadn't been to the cash machine yet that morning and I said no, and he said he had money and pulled a bunch of dollar bills out of his pocket that were all kind of wadded up and sort of waved them at me.

"We pulled into a gas station and he went to the full-service pump and stuck a bandana over the tip of the barrel of the gun. He said everything was going to be all right as long as I didn't scream or make any trouble. I tried to mouth the words 'Help me' to a man standing beside the station, but all he did was wave. When the attendant put the nozzle back Jackson just drove away without giving him any money. In fact he almost caused an accident backing out of there, and then he got on I-65 north. I didn't know what he had done, but I figured it was something bad and he was going to the nearest big city, Chicago, to lose himself.

"I started babbling about my daughter and how I was afraid she would run into the street and he said she'd be all right, I had neighbors who would take care of her. Then he told me to shut up. The next thing he said was to ask if I had any aspirin, because he had a headache.

"We were riding for a long time, forty-five minutes or so, and I had my purse on my lap and in my hands were my school records for my professional-education classes, and I remember just clutching on to them and thinking I couldn't afford to lose them. He saw them and asked what they were, and I told him, and he asked what I did, and I told him my husband and I were paramedics, and he asked if we'd just started. That's about all there was of conversation. Mainly there were lots of silences. He was pretty nice and polite but seemed like he was really desperate. Most of the time, he just smoked cigarettes. He said they were after him and he had to get away. Whenever I would ask where we were going, he would just act like I hadn't said anything, he just didn't pay any attention to it.

"I was trying to study the way he looked because I wanted to be able to give a detailed description. So I was both looking at him straight and from the corner of my eye. He didn't seem to mind. He had a big bushy beard like Kenny Rogers and he had some silver paint on his face and the edge of his beard but it looked like he had tried to wipe it off.

"He drove about five miles over the speed limit. I couldn't open the door on the highway because I figured I'd die or get run over. After about an hour I read by the sign that we'd got to Frankfort, Indiana. He got off the exit and drove downtown and I got really scared because he seemed more unsure of himself and frightened. I was studying him coming up to stop signs and getting the rhythm of the way he did it, and finally I waited until he was stopped and looking in the other direction and just opened the door and leaned against it and fell out. He tried to grab me but missed and drove away. He ran over my right leg, and I could tell it was broken. Where I fell out was in front of a car wash and someone from it ran over to me and I told him my leg was broke and not to move me, because usually they try to stand you up and brush you off.

"I never cried the whole time, but after I heard what he did, I burst out in tears."

JACKSON DROVE through Frankfort until he came to a trailer park. He stopped in front of one of the trailers. A woman inside looking out of a window saw him coming toward her. He was wearing the trenchcoat and had the gun concealed beneath it. The woman had a three-year-old boy, who'd been badly burned a few weeks before when a gas grill exploded. The boy had just got out of the hospital, and when the woman saw Mike leaving his car and walking toward her trailer she took him to be a man from a social agency which had been helpful to the boy while he was being treated. She thought she should prepare for her visitor, so she went into the bathroom to see how she looked. When she came out, Jackson was standing in her living room. Her son had answered the door. Jackson told her he wanted the keys to her car and told her to collect her son and come with him. She said he could have all her money and the keys but she didn't want to go with him, and he told her she had to. The boy sat in the front seat between them. Mike kept the shotgun between his legs, the barrel pointed at the floor. As they drove, the woman begged Mike to let her and the boy out. The boy had an appointment at the hospital. Mike didn't answer, but he patted the boy on his leg and said, "Tell your mommy everything's going to be all right." Outside town they passed a crew of men at work on the road. "Don't signal them," Mike told her. "Don't try anything." She told him she wasn't about to jump out of the car with her son still in it. After driving for ten or twelve minutes, they had arrived in the country. Jackson pulled to the side of the road. He took the woman's money and three rings she was wearing, then let her and her son leave the car. They walked toward some woods. The woman had no shoes; there had not been time to get them, or her glasses. She held her son by the hand and watched Mike drive across the horizon in her car.

AROUND SIX THAT EVENING—that is, about eight hours later—he drove into the parking lot of a shopping mall in Clayton, Missouri, a suburb of St. Louis, two hundred and fifty miles southwest of Indianapolis. A woman who crossed his path says, "It happened at the end of the day in broad daylight. I was trying to get my son out of the car, and he was involved with doing something with the visors and wouldn't get out, and I had my hands full with him and I didn't pay Jackson any heed. I saw him from the corner of my eye—he was pulled up in front of an entrance to the mall, but not a main one—and I thought he was letting someone out. I was fussing with my son. Jackson was standing by his car and he turned toward me and said, 'Give me your purse.' And the first time he said it, he didn't really have my attention—he said it in a very soft voice—then he said it again. He was about six feet from me the first time and he took about two steps closer and I saw he was holding a shotgun, and the sight of it just sort of stunned me, I didn't really take it in. What went through my mind is that part in *Superman* where Clark Kent and Lois Lane come out of the Daily Planet Building and some guy in the alley beside it tells Lois he wants her purse, and she throws it to the side, but right away the look on his face made me realize he was really serious. It was kind of quiet somehow, but intense and not nice. The second time he spoke and I looked at him, he really captured my attention. I had been an assistant prosecutor and I knew that this guy had a look that was familiar and that he was in no mood for conversation, that it wouldn't do any good to try to talk him out of it, or resist, or maybe even say anything. I was just concerned for the safety of my son, and I was really scared, but I thought, This isn't the movies, this is real, just try to appear as calm as you can and don't do anything that would make him nervous. Which isn't easy to do when you're that scared.

I really worried that he was going to make me get into my car and go somewhere with him, but I think he saw that I was having trouble with my son, that I was a mother with a kid, and that was maybe more than he wanted to take on. I tossed him the purse, very gently, without any tricks. He had taken a step back and was about six feet away. Then he made me and my son get out of the car and he said, 'Lie down,' and I got down on my hands and knees, lower, actually, right almost to the ground, but I was instinctively trying to keep my clothes from getting dirty, I guess, and that wasn't good enough for him. He pointed the gun at us and told us to lie all the way down. He said if we moved, we were gone. He walked over to his car and I kept my head down—I wasn't taking any chances—so I never even saw which direction he left in."

A FEW WEEKS before Mike Jackson's rampage, a man named Earl Dallas Finn, forty-seven and a welder, dreamed of his parents and an uncle, who were dead. They were coming to get him, and the effect of the dream was to make him feel that his own end was near. Telling one of his daughters about it he said, "If it's your time, it's your time. There isn't anything you can do."

Finn was the only child born of older parents who had been told they couldn't have children. Their friends gave the baby the nickname Mickey, after the sedative drops, because they thought he was a knockout. He married when he was eighteen and his wife was fourteen. They had three daughters and a son.

As a young man, Finn found work as a cook, which he loved, but it didn't pay well enough, and he gave it up. He would sometimes say that when his kids were grown he was going back to it. On the birthdays of his children he would fix their favorite dishes, such as Baked Alaska. Among his effects was a notebook of recipes, mostly in French.

On September 22, Finn had worked late to collect overtime. He usually shared a ride to work, and wasn't planning to drive on this day, but the man he would have gone with didn't care to work extra hours, so Finn took his own car. Around a quarter of seven that evening, as he was travelling along Interstate 70, through St. Peters, Missouri, twenty-five miles west of St. Louis, he either drew alongside Mike Jackson, or Mike Jackson drew alongside him. Perhaps he looked over at Mike. Finn was wearing a blue shirt of a shade resembling a policeman's. His Ford LTD was a model commonly used by police departments. Jackson aimed the barrel of his shotgun toward Finn and fired through the cars' open windows from four feet away. Other drivers on the interstate heard a boom which made them think someone had blown out a tire and saw Finn's car leave the highway and crash into a light pole. No one recalled the car Jackson was driving. The violence of the crash was such that the police concluded that the wound to Finn's head was a result of the force of its impact.

AFTER HE SHOT Earl Finn, Jackson drove ten miles west on the interstate to O'Fallon. He left the highway and found his way to the parking lot of a grocery store.

"I was walking out of the IGA with a grocery bag," says a woman who met him there. "I'm very—what do you call the word? I guess, 'intuitive'? And I had a feeling earlier that evening to keep mobile. It was just a strange evening.

I had left my job without my purse. I found this out because I was doing an errand after work—I had some family pictures in my briefcase—and I was dropping them off at the Northeast Mall, which was in a very transitional part of town, and I discovered I didn't have my purse, so I went back to work, and I didn't have my keys, which were in the purse, so I had to get security to let me in. I felt strange all the way back, and I said a small prayer for myself and for my daughter to be safe, and for my car, I guess not to have an accident. I had been visiting some family the weekend before and I was talking to my nephew about violent things happening in the world, and I said that in small towns violence doesn't happen often but when it *does*, it tends to be sudden and barbaric. So I was praying not to let that happen. When I got my purse, it was too late to go back to leave off my film, so I went to the IGA. I parked beside a car with the hood up, and there was a man helping the man who was driving to see what was wrong—I guess it had overheated—and who was in the car was Jackson. I went into the store, and when I came out I had only one bag—again, stay mobile—and I had put it on the fender of my car on the passenger's side while I unlocked the door, and when I did I saw the man in the car next to me make a small movement with his arm, opening the door. He started this slow circle around the back of my car, and when he turned the corner of the fender he started coming toward me real fast. My eyes were on him and he knew, I just had that extra bit of awareness. It's not that I froze; there wasn't time to run. But he knew I saw him, and he sped up as he turned the corner. He had on this blue trenchcoat, and the gun was underneath it, and I was turning to face him. He stepped up and grabbed my arm. He told me to get into the car, and I was struggling and no one was helping. There were people around—I guess they were thinking it was a family fight—and people scattered. I started shouting. He didn't seem to like that, he flinched. I think he was tired and scared and he just wanted to get away. He said, 'Get in the car.' I think what saved my life is there was a kid in a truck who was watching and I don't think he saw the gun. Jackson was keeping it most of the time under his coat, holding it down against his leg, and people told me later he pointed it at my face for a moment, and someone else said he saw it pointed at my stomach, but all I ever remember seeing was the barrel of it under his coat. But this kid got out of the truck and came up, and then he saw the gun and backed off, but he was shouting for help and for someone to get the police. I was backing off and moving up a small slope behind me and one of my shoes came off, and I guess I lost my balance and fell backward.

"It was five to seven when I came out of the store. I know that because I always arranged with my daughter that when I was going to be home after seven, I would call, so she wouldn't be worried, and I knew that I hadn't.

"Anyway, I fell over and decided I would take a beating, I would be killed, I would take whatever was going to happen, but I wasn't going to get in that car and be kidnapped and my daughter never knowing where I was or what happened to me, I just would have disappeared. And I felt as if Jackson had a moment of, I don't know, empathy. He was looking at me and back at the kid screaming, and he kept looking back and forth, his head was just flipping back and forth, I think he was disoriented.

"I put my hands over my stomach because I thought he was going to shoot me there, or at least I thought he would beat me with the gun. I said, 'If you have the nerve to shoot me in front of all these people, then do it.' He turned back and forth, then he said very softly, 'Just give me the keys.' I threw them down the slope and they landed on the pavement and skidded under the car. He reached down and got them. He was almost gentle at that moment, I thought, docile, and that was a strange thing, because later the police kept describing an aggressive-type man and when I said I thought he was docile, they thought maybe they didn't have the right man and I hadn't seen Jackson at all.

"He drove off in my car and my briefcase was in it and that had my checkbook and my address book and for a moment I watched him drive off and I was kind of in a state of awe, because I still had my purse and I wondered why he didn't take that. Someone grabbed me then and took me inside. I was standing there and my shoe was still outside and all of a sudden I was hysterical because I thought he would go to my home—he had my address on the checks—and take my daughter. I didn't know who he was, I mean I didn't know where he had come from, I didn't know what had gone on all day, and it didn't occur to me that he might be from out of town. I just assumed he knew where he was.

"The next day the security man who had let me in at work was white as a sheet. He said, 'I would have been the last one to see you.'"

The young man in the pickup says, "Jackson pulled in and his car was overheating—it was steam coming out— and he pulled in kind of slow and I watched him get out the driver's side and he was looking at me, studying me real close. He was kind of hobo-like in appearance, and he got out and fixed the back of his coat, it was a trenchcoat and I thought he was fussing with the belt, but maybe he did have a pistol back there—the F.B.I. guy kept asking me did I see a handgun—but I didn't. Anyway, he walked around the back of his car and opened the passenger's side, and I figured he was getting some deposit bottles and that's when I saw the shotgun—he was sticking it under his coat, and I could just see about six inches of the barrel below the hem of his trenchcoat. Right away I was thinking: robbery. And then he turned and was looking right at me. I reached over and switched off the radio—I guess because it was a disturbance—and put my hand on the door to get out. And then I realized I left the keys in the car, so I opened the door and pulled them out, because it was my dad's truck and I wasn't going to let this guy take it. I grabbed a pop bottle from inside the cab and I was emptying it out and it was taking forever to drain—I turned it upside down and I was shaking the soda out—I guess I was thinking I would throw it at him. And that's when the woman came out of the store, and as soon as she did, he saw her, and he went straight for her. He grabbed her and I started shouting, 'Let her go!' and I was yelling, 'He's got a gun!' and this woman pulled up next to them and got out of her car with her daughter and started walking toward the store and I said, 'Lady, get out of here, he's got a gun!' and she just walked around the other side of the woman's car and into the store and went shopping. And I was yelling and no one was stopping, the traffic's just going back and forth, everybody's just going home, and he just kept looking back and forth,

back and forth at me, then her, me, then her, and I'm
shouting, 'Someone call the police!' I had moved up close
to him, maybe about ten feet away and he turned right
toward me with the gun—he had it out now, he brought
it out when the woman came out of the store—and I knew
he could have shot me, but I wasn't really thinking about
it at the time, it was more like this was unreal, it wasn't
really happening. I remember thinking that he could shoot
either of us. The woman had on this white dress, with little
black marks, but mostly white, and I remember looking at
it and seeing it all go red in my mind. But he didn't shoot.
I heard him say, 'Get in the car,' and the woman was re-
peating what he was saying, except disagreeing, like, 'No,
I'm not getting in the car.' She was screaming, but he wasn't
raising his voice or anything, he was real clear, real calm,
keeping his voice low, like he didn't want a scene, and I
heard him say, 'Just give me the keys,' and she threw them,
and he turned back at me, and it was like he never really
took his eyes off me the whole time he was bending over
to pick them up, except for just an instant to see where the
keys were, and then he got into the car and backed up real
hard. And I was thinking the whole time I could block him
in, I could block his car with my truck, or block the exit,
but I kept thinking that he'd get out anyway, and also my
brother was in the store and I was scared he'd come out
while this was going on, and I was afraid that if those electric
doors opened up suddenly Jackson would get spooked and
start shooting. When he backed up, I was getting ready to
throw the bottle, but it's funny how your mind works, I
was thinking, if I break his windshield, I'm going to have
to pay for it. I don't know really what I would have done.

If he'd shot her, I was going to charge him, try and pin him against the wall of the store. Anyway, he pulled out real fast onto the street and I went running up and ran alongside the car—I think I even touched the door as he was pulling away—and his eyes were just locked on me the whole time, just a cold, dead stare. Cold and hateful and dead."

JACKSON DROVE the woman's car up and down the streets of O'Fallon for five minutes, until he came to a house with a yard where an older man was planting a tree. A woman who was inside the house says, "I had come to pick up my daughter after school at my mother's house and my grandfather was visiting from Minnesota and he was out planting a tree in the yard, and he said he noticed Jackson coming up driving this woman's car—he came up real slow and was looking at him and then he went up the block and turned around and came back—but my grandfather didn't pay him too much attention. We had three cars in the driveway—my grandfather's, mine, and my mother's. Jackson parked and got out and left the engine running and the door open, and he came up to my grandfather, and he said, 'Give me the keys to your car.' He had on this blue raincoat, and I guess he hid the gun under it when he walked up to my grandfather, but he brought it out when he spoke. My grandfather said he didn't have the keys, although he did, and Jackson patted his pockets but he didn't happen to find them, so Jackson took my grandfather inside, marched him right in. I guess he said, 'Let's go get the keys,' and Grandpa came to the sliding door and I heard him calling, 'Shirley, Shirley,' for my mother, but she was down in the basement doing laundry and never heard him. I had taken some extra-strength Tylenol because I had a headache, and was lying down in another room and I heard my grandfather's voice and there was something wrong in it, and I thought, Now why isn't she answering him, so I got up because I was worried for him and went into the other room and said, 'Grandpa, what's the matter, are you okay?' and he said, 'This man wants the keys to your car.'

"And my purse was on the table between us and next to it were the keys and I didn't know what was going on. Jackson had the shotgun down by his side and I wasn't paying that much attention to it—I thought it was a cane. He was sweating so hard the sweat was just dripping off his beard and falling on the floor—he was drenched—and I said, 'What's wrong, have you had an accident, do you need to go to the hospital,' and he brought the gun up and into my face and said, 'Get in the car.' I just said, 'Okay, okay.' We started out the door and I got ahead of him, my grandfather was behind, so we were on both sides of him, which I guess scared him, and I had my hair pulled back in a barrette, and he grabbed my hair and pulled it so hard he pulled a hank of it out. I always keep the passenger door locked and there were bucket seats and a stick shift, so I knew for me to get into the car he was going to have to get in first and lean across, but I had no plans for getting in. He was standing there and saying, 'Get in,' and he had the gun right in my face, but I wasn't going to get in. I didn't want to be raped and killed or whatever he was going to do to me. I didn't do anything heroic, but I thought if I was going to get killed, it was going to be right there. When he went round to the driver's side he turned his back and I just ran back to the house. My daughter was out walking the dog and she came up the street just as he left. He passed right by her and we watched him go up the road as I called the police."

As it happened, the woman's husband was on his way to meet her. "I was coming into town," he says, "and I saw my car go by. It was an Eighty-five Buick Regal and there weren't too many around, so I was pretty sure it was mine, and I figured this guy had stolen it from a lot. I turned my truck around, and took off after the car. He was on his way out into the country going about eighty miles an hour and forcing people off the road and I hung back about a quarter of a mile—I couldn't see the license plate or anything. He kept going and finally I lost him—the traffic was flying by and it was crazy to keep up with him. I began to think it wasn't my car anyway. I'd chased him about ten miles, and I was far enough out in the country that I decided I would just head home—I was closer to my house than my mother-in-law's—and I thought I'd just call them from there and see what had happened.

"In about two or three minutes, though, he comes back, he must have turned around because he thought he was getting too far out in the country, and this time I saw the license plate and I turned around again. I got up behind him then and I was thinking of cutting him off, or maybe putting him into the ditch to get the car, and I got up about ten feet from the back bumper and that's when he turned the shotgun toward me and pulled the trigger and blew out the back window. All the glass and pellets just came *flying* toward me and that's when I eased off. Right where you come back into O'Fallon, he passed a cop going the other way with his lights flashing, and I figured the cop would

get him, but he was on his way to my mother-in-law's—
the last place they knew he'd been—and I guess he never
seen him."

JACKSON DITCHED THE BUICK near the parking lot of
an apartment complex in O'Fallon. He saw a young man
polishing a Cadillac in the parking lot. He walked toward
him, and when he got within ten feet he pulled the shotgun
from under his coat and told the man to get into the car.
Jackson drove the Cadillac to the highway, travelled about
four miles west, then took an exit south, into the country.
He told the man that he was going to kill him. At a gas
station he handed money for sandwiches to the pump attendant, who went into the station, which had a snack bar,
and brought the sandwiches back. He gave one of them to
his passenger. Each time he lit a cigarette he offered the
young man one. But he said again that he was going to kill
him. In the backseat of the Cadillac was a child's seat for
the young man's daughter. Jackson did not say much, but
the young man talked about his daughter, in the hope that
the subject would soften him. Jackson said, "Don't look at
me, and be quiet." He drove slowly. It had got dark. When
the headlights of other cars approached or came up behind
them, he would pull to the side of the road and wait for
the car to pass.

Bill Burgess, Chief of Police of Wright City, a town
fourteen miles west of O'Fallon: "I was listening to the
scanner—I got about six or seven police channels on it—
and I could hear them talking they were looking for an
individual who disappeared with a car up in O'Fallon. He
could have gone anywhere. I knew they had the manhunt

over in O'Fallon for the guy who shot the probation officer in Indianapolis, but I didn't know that the man who stole the car necessarily was the same one. So me and my deputy were just sitting up by the bridge above the highway waiting for it, in case it come our way. While I was sitting, though, I got a call for some kind of disturbance—tires squealing or people shouting, I can't really remember—but I could see when I got there it had been cleared up; I didn't even have to get out of the car, so I just went back to the bridge. The call only took a short while, and by the time I took care of it, he should have come and gone, but he had messed around on some backroads up there in St. Steven's County and that held him up. And if I wasn't there he probably would have killed that lady that works in our service station by the highway where he turned off, high-strung as she was, and that was his way of doing it, because he didn't have no money, or he had three dollars or something.

"I knew it was the car right away when I saw it—we had a very detailed description—but there was only one person in it, the driver, and we had been told he'd taken the owner of the car hostage. He came up the exit ramp and turned into the Sunoco station, and went back of it and come out the other side. He saw us right when he came off the ramp. And I moved the patrol car across the road, so I could keep him in view. I wasn't going to arrest him, I was just going to observe him, maybe tail him till I could get a backup. I had the license plate, and we confirmed that real quick. I was driving, and my deputy was sitting beside of me, and I was expecting Jackson to get out at the service station, but instead he drew up to us and levelled the barrel of that gun on his window and pulled the trigger. I say he levelled it, but I never saw the gun, he just had it with the tip of the barrel sticking out the window, and I'll tell you something—I never heard the blast, either. I guess it was muffled by the inside of the car. I saw the flash, but I never heard the blast. The flash was just like you take your cigarette lighter and fire it up, so it could have been that, to my eye, I mean, you couldn't really tell, and he let it go at an angle to us, just as he was pulling up. My deputy was about getting his gun out the window and was going to tell him he was a police officer when that shot came. He got off two shots, and then he fell back in the seat and said, 'I've been hit,' and you could see there was blood running down his forehead, but I couldn't see the wound because it was up under his hair. So I squeezed off four shots at Jackson as he was taking off. I was out of the car, arm raised to draw him in my sight, and dancing around at the same time, because I didn't know if he'd shoot again, or *what* was going on.

"After he had went past I drew a good bead on his rear window, and I was squeezing off on that when I realized there were some houses down there beside of him, and if we had a ricochet you don't know what could have happened.

"With my deputy hit and my not knowing what was going on with that, I didn't take off after him. I didn't really have no backup here, but it just happened that there was a sheriff coming down the interstate, that was just luck, he saw Jackson on the service road going *along*, and he come down from the highway and went up the service road after him. The service road runs straight beside the interstate till you come a couple miles up there to a rest area, then it begins to turn away from the highway, and I guess Jackson realized he wasn't going to make it back to the interstate that way, so he just pointed the Cadillac toward the highway and went right through the fence behind the rest area. He hit that fence at about a hundred miles an hour. Went over some deep ditches and just tore the radiator and the transmission out, banged down on the road and went into the median. The sheriff come along, and I guess he saw that fence tore up and he went back behind the rest area to try to catch up to him, so he lost him for a while, and I guess the Cadillac car was steaming up from taking out the radiator and Jackson figured it was going to die, he knew the ride was over, so he ditched it.

"Time we got to the car we didn't really know which way he had gone—that's some pretty bushy country up there—and about right away it commenced to downpour, a terrible hard rain, and I'll tell you what, he just simply disappeared."

NANCY GAHL

THE INDIANAPOLIS POLICEMEN who arrived at Mike's house in response to the report of a shooting did not immediately learn the name of the man who lay on the sidewalk. They were required to wait for the coroner before they could touch the corpse. Having knelt beside him and found his wallet and badge, one of them called Tom's office, and Tom's boss and another probation officer came to the house. By the time they arrived, Tom's body had been taken to the morgue. The two men looked briefly through the house, and then they drove out to tell Nancy.

Nancy had called her husband at his office around nine-thirty. She wanted to hear his voice. All she learned from her call was that he was not at his desk. Had she happened to turn on the radio she might have heard of the murder that morning of a probation officer whose name the announcer was pronouncing "Tommy Galt," instead of Tom E. Gahl.

Nancy was on the telephone in the kitchen with a friend when she heard the knock on her door. It was about eleven. She was by herself in the house. She put the phone down on the counter and went to answer the door. When she saw who was waiting and their somber expressions, she said the first thing that came to her mind.

"Is he dead?"

Tom's boss said, "Let us in," and once they were inside she said again, "Is he dead?" and he said, "Yes."

She found her way back to the kitchen and sat down. Tom's boss saw the phone off the hook and picked it up and explained what had happened and then hung it up. One of the men asked Nancy if she didn't think it would be a good idea to call her parents. She said, "Yeah, that's a good idea," and she did it and sat back down. Then one of the men asked if she shouldn't call Tom's parents, and she said, "Yeah, that's a good idea," and she did and sat down again. She felt as if her mind and her body had simply closed down. Then her stomach began to churn, "as if it were rebelling against what the mind was saying," she later recalled, and she felt that she had to go into the bathroom. And there, of course, was the towel Tom had dried himself with that morning after jogging. It was where he had hung it, it was still damp, and its presence seemed more than her mind could take in. How could what they were saying be true, she thought, if his towel is still here?

Her pastor arrived. So did the chaplain who worked for the police department. He apologized for not having delivered word of Tom's death; he said he was held up by other responsibilities. Nancy was happier to have learned from someone she knew. She told the chaplain she wanted to see

Tom in the morgue, and he discouraged her. She pressed him, but he continued to say he didn't think it would be a good idea. In frustration she turned to her pastor and asked why they wouldn't let her see him, and then something just clicked in her mind, and she said, "Was he shot in the head?" and the pastor said, "Yes."

NICHOLAS, FOUR, arrived home on the school bus. Then Nancy and Nicholas and the pastor went to Christopher's school. Nancy was known to the people who worked at the school as a parent who often volunteered, and when she asked in the office to see Christopher, the woman she spoke to asked if something was wrong.

"I said that Tom had just been shot and killed, and the woman started shaking," she recalls.

Christopher was on the playground. The tone of voice of the teacher who sent him to the office made him wonder if he had done something wrong. Then he began to worry that something had happened to his mother; he thought maybe she had been in a car accident. When he got to the office and she knelt down and told him, he didn't cry. He clenched his fists, and then he said, "Daddy?" Then he said it again. The effect of the shock was to produce in him a kind of exalted state. He said that when he died he was going to tell his father everything that had happened in his life, and what kind of person he had been, and what he had accomplished.

That afternoon a reporter from the paper came to Nancy's door. Nancy wondered why the paper was interested in her family's story—that is, against all that had gone on, her own feelings and the events of her day seemed inconsequential

—but she sat in the living room and talked to the woman. When the afternoon's edition arrived, "I saw the headline," she says, "and I saw some of the details, and I knew it was about us, but I didn't really know how to take it in."

Christopher found himself shooting baskets through the hoop his father put up for him, first at a height his small frame could manage, then at the one the rules called for. A neighbor's boy, home early from school, passed by and said, "What are you doing here? You're playing hookey," and Christopher said, "My father was shot and killed this morning."

Throughout the day friends and relatives arrived— Nancy's father, her mother-in-law, a brother from California, neighbors who came to express their sorrow. Before her family got there her pastor did what he could to shield her, but finally she said that she needed to be alone with her children. Her pastor asked if she was sure and she said that she was. Then everyone left and Nancy and Christopher and Nicholas sat upstairs on her bed and held each other and tried to understand what had happened to them.

When she went to bed that night she put her face to the pillow and found the scent of her husband. She thought of how they would embrace in the darkness before sleep. She thought of all the plans she and Tom had for raising the boys and for growing old together, and she felt a terrible sadness. It seemed to her that her mind was like an engine racing, as if the pain had a will and momentum of its own. She kept returning in her imagination to the place where Tom died and trying to figure out how it had happened. What did Jackson say? Did he say anything? Did Tom have any warning? She would run through every aspect of it she could think of and when she finished, she would start all over again, with some variation. Did Tom know he was going to die? Did he run? Was Jackson chasing him? Had he stalked him? Then: Did Jackson know Tom was coming? Did he know he would kill him? *When* had he decided to kill him? Was he going to kill someone else and had Tom only appeared at the wrong moment?

Now and then during the night she thought she could hear Christopher sighing in his bed in his room down the hall. She thought of going to him, then held back, thinking, He's asleep, don't disturb him. Later he told her that he heard her, and thought of coming in, but decided she was probably asleep and that he shouldn't wake her.

At five she got up and went downstairs and turned on the television. And saw Tom's body on the sidewalk, covered by a sheet.

Around six, she went back up to bed, and found Tom's shorts and the T-shirt he'd worn to go running. She picked them up and held them to her face, thinking, How can this be, I can still smell him here, he can't be gone. The deep, heaving tears she wept woke her brother, who came in and sat next to her on the bed and put his arm around her and cried too.

She went downstairs again around eight and called the office of the lawyer who handled Tom's and her affairs. No one answered, so she called him at home. His wife said cheerfully, "Oh, hi, Nancy," and Nancy asked to speak to her husband. When he came on, he said, "What's up?" Nancy said, "I guess you haven't read the papers or heard the news." He said, "No, what's happened?" and she said,

"Tom was shot and killed." The long silence that followed was broken finally by his saying, "Oh, Nancy, I didn't know." She explained that she was calling because she was uncertain about what happened with her money, whether it was tied up, and whether she faced some additional difficulty, and he told her he would take care of all of it for her.

Then the phone rang and it was her doctor, asking if she was all right, and saying he would phone in a prescription to help her rest.

THAT AFTERNOON she opened her door to a policeman who placed in her hands Tom's wallet and his wedding ring—each in a plastic bag with a case number written on it—and his briefcase with the same number written on the side in chalk.

THE HOUSE was full of people. Tom's brother from D.C. arrived. Friends brought food. Others appeared simply because they felt the need to be there with Nancy and the boys. Most didn't really know what to say—Nancy would open the door and they'd fall into her arms—but it meant a great deal to her that they came. Nevertheless, there were moments when she felt overwhelmed and needed to be alone. She kept feeling that if she could just get outside and away from the activity of the house she could take stock of her thoughts and place them in order. She didn't want the people who'd come to see her to feel she had turned her back on them, and she thought of going upstairs to her bedroom, but the bedroom was too lonely a place for her now, so she opened the front door to step out, and there was one of her friends from church with cleaning buckets in her hands. "I just had to come and see you," the woman said. "I don't know what to say, but I had to be here. Do you mind if I wash your windows?"

Nancy decided to have Tom buried in Valparaiso, in northern Indiana, where he had grown up. As a resting place, it struck her as safe, whereas Indianapolis did not. A difficulty arose over when he could be buried. The coroner had called for an autopsy, but there was the question of when he could find time to perform it. A friend of the family who had influence with the coroner called his office, and the autopsy was scheduled for Tuesday morning. The coroner would release the body that afternoon; the burial could take place on Wednesday.

A man at the funeral home called when Tom's body arrived, and said it would be several hours before they could make the body presentable. Nancy didn't know what was left of Tom that she would recognize, but she knew she needed to see some part of him. "I don't care if it's even just the hand," she told them. "I need to see something."

The man called around four and told her she should bring them the clothes she wanted Tom to be buried in. She said there was no need for clothes, because no one would see him in his casket. With her father and Tom's mother, her brother, and the boys, she went to see him. Her pastor met them at the funeral home and said he had already been in and that Tom didn't look too bad, and that was the first time Nancy realized his head was still there.

Tom lay on a table at the far end of a dimly lit room, covered to his neck by a pale-blue shroud. His head rested on a pillow and was turned slightly to his right. Viewed from the side that was unharmed, he looked like himself, but from straight on his features were altered by his skin's being stretched toward his wounds to conceal them. Around the edge of that side of his forehead Nancy saw small cuts and scrapes from where his head struck the pavement. He wasn't wearing his glasses—the police had them—and the funeral home had parted his hair on the wrong side, but as she stood there, the thought was borne in on her, It's Tom, it really is Tom. She walked around him. She leaned over and stroked his hair and Christopher did so too. She held Nicholas up to look at him. Then she leaned over to touch her nose to his and that was when she discovered he no longer smelled like her husband.

Seeing Tom's body gave Nancy and the boys a peculiar sense of relief. Christopher said, "I feel better now." Tom had been torn from them and was now in some way returned, and perhaps it was the shock of their grief and suffering that protected them, but in some obscure way it made all of them feel eased of a burden.

After they had taken in the sight of the shroud and his face and his oddly parted hair, the pastor called them together in a corner of the room and led them in a prayer. Then Nancy took her last look at her husband. She stayed by his side for what she recalls as only a moment. She wishes now she had seen more of his body. She wishes she had touched his hand. What stopped her was an awareness of all the other people in the room. Not until later did it occur to her that she might have asked for a moment alone. Instead, she felt that everyone was there to support her, and a request that they leave her might strike them as thoughtless. She worried also that they might think her wish to be alone with his body was morbid. And she didn't want to keep them waiting.

The salesman from the funeral home took Nancy to the room where they kept their caskets. In a voice lowered almost to a whisper he told her that any money she saved on a coffin could be put toward the future of the boys.

The sleep she managed that night came with the help of a sedative.

"WEDNESDAY MORNING the hearse came by the house to pick us up," Nancy says. "We had three cars making the trip. We drove the two and a half hours to Valparaiso, and since the hearse driver was from Indianapolis and didn't know the way to the cemetery, our car led them at the end. I just wanted to have the family at the burial, to say goodbye. I hadn't had the hour or the place of the ceremony published in the paper, but when we turned into the cemetery there were about two hundred people—people who'd known Tom growing up, relatives, and friends who found out about the service and came all the way from Indianapolis. We drove up and they were all peering in the windows, looking at me, and their faces were just ashen. We got out and people came up saying how sorry they were. I could see the faces of people I knew on the fringes of the crowd, but a lot of people I just didn't even recognize. Finally everyone walked away to the gravesite. The service went by so quickly, it was over in no time. Pastor gave a beautiful sermon, and then you threw a few handfuls of dirt on the grave. Then I was alone with Tom in his casket, and I don't even remember what went through my mind. Honey, I love you. Goodbye."

―――――――

NANCY AND THE BOYS spent Wednesday night in Valparaiso and left for home Thursday morning around eight. She stopped at a McDonald's restaurant along the way where she and Tom always let the boys run, and sat there in a storm of memories. When she got home she saw the pastor and told him she was having a really hard time and he took her into his office and they cried together.

FRIDAY A SERVICE WAS HELD for Tom in a church downtown. Hundreds attended. Many were forced to wait outside or in a room where a speaker was wired to broadcast the service. From the front pew, Nancy and Nicholas and Christopher heard the pastor tell the mourners, "What shall we say to this horrendous crime that took Tom from us? Where was God when Tom needed him?"

Nancy stood for three hours in the receiving line, time after time recovering her composure, only to see someone approach from the corner of her eye who would cause her to weep all over again.

ON MONDAY she woke and watched the hands of the clock approach five after eight and then pass. With Christopher and her father and her brother, she went downtown to clean out Tom's office. On the day that he was killed the door was closed, and his office left more or less as it had been. The files of his cases had been removed, and the pages of his notebook that dealt with the business of the department were gone, but his calendar still hung on the wall with his appointments noted and the paydays marked off, and the pictures of his family still met the eyes of anyone sitting in his chair. He might almost have been expected at any moment, except for the wreath on the door.

They took the pictures down from the walls and emptied the drawers of his desk. Nancy's father lost her mother, to cancer, when she was only forty-seven. So it was natural that it was toward him Nancy turned to ask, "How long will it hurt this way?"

THAT AFTERNOON they left Christopher off at school, during the noon recess, just exactly where he'd been called from a week before. He hadn't wanted to ride the bus that morning and have everyone lapse into silence when he climbed aboard. Nancy watched while his friends came over and took him in. Some time later he told her he believed that the first period of their mourning was easier for him than for her, because he had his friends to distract him, whereas she had just to sit home by herself and be sad.

EVERYONE STAYED as long as they could. The second Friday night was Nancy's first alone with the boys. Around nine a hard rain started to fall. She went to bed and by midnight she was back downstairs trying to stop the rush of water flooding underneath the patio door. The room had flooded a few weeks before and she had just had the furniture repaired and the rug shampooed. The towels she held to the bottom of the door made no difference in the flood, and before long she was leaning against the door and crying, knowing Tom would have dug a trench to deflect the water, or swept it away from the door, or figured some way to defeat it. She felt as if a new journey had begun and she hadn't asked for it, or wanted it, and she couldn't have felt more alone. Finally she just gave up and went to bed.

In the middle of the night, Christopher rose to go to the bathroom. He walked to the door of his room and looked down the hall and sensed in its shadows something forbidding that he'd never been aware of before. He returned to his bed, and that was the first time he recalls ever feeling afraid of the dark.

NANCY HAD BEEN AWARE that the police were searching for Jackson in Missouri and that he hadn't been found. She kept the television on. Occasionally she saw the image of his mother, asking Mike to surrender, or his brother Jimmy surrounded by reporters, so she knew that Jackson had family, but much more than that she didn't take in. She was too involved in what was happening to her and the boys to think at any length about Jackson. After a few days she began to feel that an account of the search would be a document the boys and she might someday want, so she started to clip articles from the paper and record the news from her television. The image of Jackson that appeared most frequently behind the shoulders of television anchors and at the heads of columns of newspaper type was taken in prison in 1985, when his particular obsession with grooming had been subdued by some other passion. Christopher and Nicholas found this version of him terrifying. "His hair was wild, his eyes were wild, he didn't look human," says Nancy. "He looked more like an animal to me."

A couple of weeks after the murder an agent from the F.B.I. came to ask her some questions. Most of what she told him he already knew—what time Tom left the house, his concern about the visit, his brief acquaintance with Jackson, his wish that Nancy not worry. When the agent asked if there was anything else, she said, "I think if Tom knew Jackson was dangerous he wouldn't have gone."

A fund was created to receive donations toward the boys' education. Contributions arrived from classrooms, from children and their parents, from neighbors, from people who had known Tom as a child or in college or through the church or at work, from people who didn't care to identify themselves, and from probation offices all around the country. Nancy never had days when she felt like staying in bed with the curtains drawn, but she lost interest in eating. What with donations to the fund and cards and letters of sympathy, there were thousands of pieces of mail to answer. She prepared a letter of reply for strangers, who wouldn't be acquainted with her handwriting, and her friends copied out versions. Writing, "Thank you very much for your generous contribution . . . ," they sometimes completed as many as eighty letters in a day.

Friends gave her books on grieving but she had no time to read them. Struggling to arrive at some understanding of what happened, she made herself become accustomed to saying that Tom was murdered; he had not passed on, it had not been a natural way to die.

She endeavored to hold herself together for Christopher and Nicholas. She did not mind letting them see her cry— often there were moments when they all cried together— and she saw no point in pretending to strengths she didn't have, but she told her boys that they were going to make it, that she knew how to write checks, she would get them through. She told Christopher that he didn't have to occupy the place in the household his father had held; she had lived on her own before she was married. If she could do nothing else, she felt that the preservation of their sense of family and whatever portion of their childhoods remained was something she must guarantee.

Without knowing exactly what happened to Tom there seemed to Nancy no way that she could put his murder behind her. The accounts in the paper and on television were insufficiently complete. One afternoon a few weeks after the killing an agent from the FBI sat at the table in the kitchen, and by the time he left she felt she knew most of what mattered. She could close her eyes and imagine her husband with his arm at his side walking backwards and pleading with Jackson not to shoot again, and she could see Jackson bearing down on him with the shotgun. She has a scrapbook with a picture from the newspaper of Tom on the street and from the way he is lying she reconstructed how he fell. "I studied that for so long," she says. "It was all I had."

A FEW WEEKS after Tom died, Nancy had an intuition that he had left some message of farewell. She took all his clothes out of his dresser and removed the paper at the bottom of the drawers. She turned out all the pockets of his trousers and coats. She combed his shelves and the corners of his closets. And found nothing. About a month and a half after his murder, she discovered a camera that had in it a roll of pictures taken before Tom died. What she hoped was to find in it something that would ease the pain she felt over losing him, some gesture, some sign of love. To the part of her mind that gave rise to this feeling it did not seem impossible that Tom might have anticipated his end and made some effort to make it less painful. When the roll was developed, it turned out that the pictures were mainly of the boys. In the corner of one was Tom's foot.

A CASE STUDY

MIKE WAYNE JACKSON married Carolyn Long in January of 1964. They were both eighteen. The wedding took place in Indianapolis. Walking beside her up the aisle of the church, her father kept saying, "Is it too late for me to talk you out of this?" Carolyn had graduated from high school the January before and lived with her parents while she worked in a factory. Mike lived with his mother and had no job. Carolyn's father was a carpenter, and for a while he engaged Mike as a helper. He hoped that by doing so he was assuring Mike of some means of caring for his daughter, but he didn't conceal what he felt about his son-in-law. Carrying ladders and boards and passing tools back and forth, the two of them worked each other's nerves. Mike didn't like being bossed. Often he was late and occasionally he didn't show up at all. He was unskilled and learned slowly, had no stamina or discipline, was resentful of working, and, under pressure, had difficulty performing even the simplest tasks. Their arrangement lasted about two months.

Mike and Carolyn had met at a party one Friday night, when she was seventeen. She was familiar with the sight of him opening the door of his mother's car in front of the school, as a courtesy for this or that girl, and she knew what his name was, but they had never been introduced. Mike had given up classes in the ninth grade. The report cards he brought home as a boy his mother tied with a ribbon and put in a box that she keeps now in a corner of a closet. They show that he had no trouble at all with adding and subtracting or spelling or in committing to memory the capitals of the states, but that algebra, literature, and history wore him down. Toward the end he failed nearly every subject and excelled in none. He didn't like to study, and he grew impatient at the slightest difficulty. By the time he reached high school he appeared to lose interest. "It must have seemed to him as if he were in over his head," Carolyn says. At the party Mike asked Carolyn to dance. Moving slowly in place, they drew the attention of the dancers around them. From then on she was the only girl seen with her shoulder against his while he sat at the wheel of his mother's car.

She had no idea what he did all day. "I just assumed he hung out with the boys somewhere and did whatever it was that they did," she says. She knew very little about his growing up, and he never raised the subject. She expected him to take part in the kind of exchange of the past and of secret feelings that lovers enjoy, but Mike never showed any interest. You weren't supposed to ask him questions—that was the feeling he conveyed to her. The few times she asked about his childhood, he gave no answer, nor did he show any inclination to learn about hers. She knew he'd been arrested at thirteen for pointing a gun at a woman driving a taxi and taking her money, and had been sent to a juvenile home, but it didn't worry her. "I just thought everything would be fine and splendid," she says, "the way you do when you're young. I thought all trouble of that kind was behind him, and now that we were together he would live differently."

Along with the report cards in the box at the bottom of his mother's closet is a collection of pictures of Mike: as a baby; as a boy seated here and there in various years among the rows of his classmates; on a school trip to a fish hatchery near home in Mississippi; by himself holding in each hand one end of a line of fish strung like pennants across his chest; posed in the driveway in front of the bumper of the family car. The record of his childhood written by his mother in a baby book and on the backs of pictures includes the information that on his first birthday he received a dollar from his grandparents; that he quit Scouts to spend more time playing baseball, but instead spent so many hours by himself that his mother grew concerned; that he liked to ride his bike and collect rocks and old keys; and that his favorite song as a baby was "Silent Night, Holy Night."

He had two brothers and two sisters, all older. He was happier outside the house, in the woods or playing by the stream banks or riding his bike on roads through fields that led into the country. He liked to use his imagination to play and could occupy himself for hours. He loved animals and was frightened by the sight of his mother killing chickens for their table. As a boy he impressed one of his sisters as too fragile. "He had no protection in him," she recalls. "No way of recovering from a setback, it was all just too raw. He couldn't take the shocks. He'd get knocked down and he couldn't get back up that easily." If Mike had been inclined to discuss his growing up, he might have told Carolyn that his father was in the habit of telling him he was not his child. His father had been a blacksmith in Mississippi, then brought his family to Indianapolis in search of better work. He was considered to have a good head for business but to have wasted his talents because of drinking. He seemed to his children to be away as often as he was home. He would sometimes make remarks about the developing body of one of his daughters and let his friends do the same, and the girl felt he should have protected her from that. He worked a trash route for a while, and he would sometimes take one of Mike's brothers with him. Along the way he would stop at bars where he knew women. He was not faithful to his wife. When he drank he was liable to lose his temper.

Mike's mother was determined and strong-willed and did what she could to protect him. She also insisted he attend church. When he came to tell her of some accomplishment, she would say, "You could have done better." Carolyn grew to feel that Mike had in him a streak of the con man, and that he developed it as a means of concealing the facts of his life from his mother while trying to give her the impression he was exactly the son she wished him to be.

Mike's father left his family when Mike was eight. He lived in an apartment that was part of a housing project, then in a trailer at a trailer park, and then in a nursing home, where he died. His family had little to do with him. Mike sometimes borrowed money from his father and never paid him back. On a night when he was hard-pressed to make any other arrangement he might end up on a couch in his father's living room. Once, when his father was gone from his trailer, Mike stole several guns and some sheets and towels and pillowcases from it. The guns he sold, and the linen he gave to girls he knew who had just moved into an apartment.

Mike rarely mentioned his father. "That was about bad times," says a friend, "and Mike was about good times." While the old man lived in the trailer park, he would carry in his pickup truck the bone from the penis of a bear. "That'd be about the first thing he showed you," says someone who knew him. "You didn't have to be talking to him no time and that would come out." As he presented it, he would say he had shot the bear out west in the woods with a twenty-two-caliber pistol.

Like any adolescent, Mike developed an affection for his image in the mirror. His skin was clear and pale. He was embarrassed by his hands, which were so small that he considered them effeminate, and kept them in his pockets.

THE WEDDING WAS PLANNED for September. Carolyn's mother was also opposed. She had no objection to Mike; she simply felt that her daughter was too young to marry. She thought Mike was polite and she liked the way he looked after his appearance.

Early one morning in the beginning of September, Carolyn's phone rang, and it was Mike's mother, saying that Mike had just been picked up by the police and charged with a rape that had taken place the night before. Mike and Carolyn had been to a drive-in movie that night. Around the time that Mike left Carolyn at her door, a man opened the passenger's side of a car stopped at an intersection a few miles from Carolyn's house. The man drew a knife and gave the woman at the wheel directions to a place where no one could see the car when they parked. The charge was sufficiently farfetched and the timing so coincidental that it never occurred to Carolyn to ask if he had done it. She went immediately to the jail, but it wasn't a visiting day and she was put off until the next one. Mike's family engaged the most highly regarded criminal lawyer in Indianapolis.

For the trial, Mike put on a dark suit, in which he appeared, seated at the defense table, handsome and blameless. He wore a white shirt and tie, his shoes were polished, his face was scrubbed, and his hair had been cut. To Carolyn he looked like someone who could never tell a lie. The trial began early in December of 1963 and lasted a week. Carolyn told the jury that Mike was with her when the rape took place. She described the affectionate life that she and Mike shared, and his lawyer pointed out that where they had spent the evening was a drive-in movie. When the plain-looking, dark-haired woman raised her right hand and told her story of trouble, Carolyn says it crossed the mind of more than one person that Mike, who was so appealing, would never have to force himself on a woman such as that. More likely, she would chase him.

The lawyer asked the woman if she saw in the courtroom the man who had raped her, and she pointed at Mike. When he asked her to find the image of her attacker among a series of photographs that included one of Mike, she chose someone else.

The trial ended late in the day. Carolyn, the lawyer,

Mike's mother, and Mike's stepfather went with friends to a restaurant near the courthouse to drink coffee and wait for the jury. They returned at two the next morning, with a verdict of not guilty, and then a number of them congratulated Mike and Carolyn on their plans to marry. Carolyn remembers that several embraced them. A few even went back to the restaurant with them.

AFTER THE WEDDING Carolyn and Mike moved into an apartment. They'd been there about a month when Mike stayed out late enough that Carolyn went to bed by herself and lay in the darkness waiting for the sound of his key in the door. Sometime after daybreak he arrived and said he was sorry, but didn't tell her where he'd been or what he'd been up to, though she asked. She grew accustomed to the sight of his back as he went out the door and to being alone at night. She began to feel that he was leading two lives. Most of the time he was back the next morning, but occasionally he stayed away longer. Carolyn pushed him to get a job—she was still working in the factory—but her being upset didn't seem to matter and after a while all he did was get angry when the subject came up. He would grow exasperated at the smallest obstacle to his plans, and his anger turned quickly into rage.

Carolyn became pregnant and was due in February of 1965. When she went into labor, she couldn't find Mike. She got herself to the hospital, and that night she gave birth to a girl. Someone found Mike, and he arrived a few hours after. Carolyn spent three days in the hospital. Eventually, she learned that where Mike had been was in bed with her best friend.

Later that winter, Mike started bringing home paintings and lamps, and storing them in the hallway and the living room. Nothing was said about where they were from or why they were there, but Carolyn assumed they were stolen. The first time two policemen showed up and asked to see the inside of their apartment, Mike wasn't home. He'd moved all the paintings and lamps out the day before.

Sometimes, in the evening, he would step out the back door of their apartment and return with the lawn chairs belonging to his neighbors. He kept them in his backyard, where a fence concealed them. When the yard overflowed, he stacked chairs in the living room. By and by he cut the webbing from the seats and backs and sold the aluminum frames for scrap.

In the spring of 1966 Carolyn became pregnant again. She left her job about two weeks before she was due, and had no money. What money Mike made he kept; it fell to Carolyn to pay the rent and the household bills. Mike didn't allow her to have visitors, and if it weren't for the time she spent among people at work she would have felt utterly isolated. A woman from work happened to come by one evening when Carolyn was alone. This was shortly before she went to the hospital. Mike came home and said to the woman, "It's time for you to go." Carolyn said, "Well, why? What's wrong, Mike? Is something the matter?" and he gave her, she says, "a look to freeze me." The woman said, "I don't see why I have to go, it's not just your house," and Mike picked her up and took her out to the street and dropped her. When he returned he threw Carolyn against the door of a closet. It was the first time he had hit her. She moved to her aunt's and went into the hospital and gave birth to a second daughter. She didn't let Mike near the child, and when she got out of the hospital she moved, with her two girls, to her mother's.

When she returned to work, she got there by taking the bus. Every morning as she got on and every evening as she got off she saw Mike in his car down the block. He never said a word, or even rolled down his window. Finally one evening he pulled up beside her and said, "Why don't you get in and talk to me," and she did, and he said all the right things and she "strolled right back to him," she says.

Carolyn, Mike, and the children moved to an apartment in a complex where the buildings had three apartments to a floor, side by side. Mike and Carolyn took over one in the middle. On either side were neighbors whose character she mistrusted. Mike fell in with them and began to act "really erratic." He'd walk out the door saying, "I'm going to Illinois," or, "I'm going to Tennessee," and she didn't have any idea where he went, but when he came back he always had money. He'd say he was sorry for leaving her alone, but no reason was given, and the state of contrition never lasted longer than a day. Shortly afterward he'd be gone again. Once he disappeared for two weeks.

Most of his money he spent on himself, but one evening she came home and found he had redecorated the apartment—"Furniture to linens and all new toys for the girls," Carolyn says. Intermittently he involved himself in the life of his family. Carolyn has a snapshot of him sitting with one of the girls. On his lap is a small plastic washtub filled with snow. The child was home sick from school, so Mike filled the washtub and made a little snowman with her. The girl has no memory of the occasion.

Not long after he redecorated the apartment, Mike was picked up by the police and held for three days. Carolyn felt that his being gone made it safe to leave. She moved in again with her aunt. When she went back to the apartment to collect her and the children's things, it was empty. Mike had taken everything in it to his mother's, so Carolyn moved in with him there. She doesn't remember what got them back together—she left and went back so many times; she thinks it was probably a phone call.

She lived with Mike and his mother, Modean, and his stepfather, Everett Embry, and Embry's twin sons. Modean would take care of the girls while Carolyn was at work. She got pregnant again, but miscarried in the middle of the night. The doctor told her to bring the fetus to a laboratory for tests. She gave it to Mike to deliver, but it never got there. "Mike cried and cried for two days," she says, "and when we asked him what happened to the fetus he said he had taken it to the lab." Carolyn assumes he buried it somewhere.

In the spring of 1967 Mike was arrested for stealing checks and for forgery. He and Carolyn had been getting along badly for months. One of her daughters says that all she remembers of her parents' marriage was the two of them standing in the kitchen and yelling at each other. Mike was sent to Michigan City, an old fortress of a prison in northern Indiana. While he was there, in 1968, Carolyn divorced him.

IN MICHIGAN CITY Mike endured for two years a punishing, thuggish, old-time prison experience, and he left the place rattled. He said very little about what happened to him there, and nothing at all about it to Carolyn, but it was clear to her and his friends he had undergone a change.

On his release he showed up at the door of Carolyn's apartment. She told him he could come in to see the girls, but couldn't stay long. He took her car and went to his mother's to collect his clothes and came back and moved in. For the next six months he was checked for drugs. After that, his daughters would sometimes see him in the bathroom with a needle in his arm.

One morning Carolyn was awakened by the pressure of something against the side of her head. She moved enough to see the barrel of a shotgun. Mike said, "I'm going to blow your head off." She said, "Honey, what's wrong?" And he said, "You know what's wrong," but she didn't. Mike held the gun against her head for perhaps ten minutes, and then he walked away. Another time as she was making his breakfast, he came into the kitchen and knocked all her canisters of sugar and flour and coffee to the floor, then made her get on her knees and clean up the mess while he held her down by the back of her neck. When she finished, he had tears in his eyes. He could be sitting there sometimes just sweet-talking her on the couch, and then take her arm and twist it behind her, and she'd say, "What's wrong?" and he'd say, "You know what's wrong," and his tone wouldn't be any different from what it had been when he was saying he loved her.

She was always leaving him and going back to her mother, then being talked into returning. During one separation he arrived at her job at the end of the day and dragged her to his car. He drove her around the city and every time she opened her mouth to ask where they were headed or what was going on he struck her with the back of his hand. He left her off at her mother's and the next morning she went to work with two black eyes and a patch above the bridge of her broken nose.

Why she tolerated what he did to her she isn't exactly sure, except that in those days, she says, you didn't as easily call the police when your husband struck you. It perhaps not only wouldn't seem like such a big deal to them, but they might almost take his side; you never knew. You just accepted the beating and went about your business. "You certainly didn't go on the Oprah show and talk about it," she says.

One morning Mike grabbed her arm and tied it with her stocking to the bedpost. He tied her legs too, even though she fought and was scared as hell besides, because she could see what he intended: the needle was beside the bed and next to it was a spoon and some matches. Mike always wanted her to use the same drugs that he did, and was infuriated by her refusing. She knew he had no idea of the potency of what he meant to inject into her veins, or its purity either, or what reaction her body would have, so she continued to fight, but stopped when the needle pierced her arm. The heroin made her drowsy, then it emptied her stomach. What she recalls of the rest of the day—it was Mother's Day—was going to her mother's in Mike's beat-up old van that he sold her car to get, and being terribly sick in the back.

MIKE DIDN'T CARE for being divorced. He kept telling Carolyn they should get married again. She would say, "Well, why, Mike? You're here and I'm here, what's the difference?" One afternoon he came home and said, "We're going after a license." That night he walked her across a field, through snow to her knees, and knocked on a preacher's door. She got married in blue jeans and without a ring. He had pawned all her rings.

Carolyn usually had a sitter look after the girls while she was at work. Once in a great while Mike would stay home and watch them, as he did one day shortly before Christmas of 1971. That evening, they planned to go shopping. When she got home, she went to the kitchen to make dinner. Mike came up behind her and put his arms around her and gave her a hug, and said, "Why don't you go upstairs and do whatever you need to get ready, and I'll make some tuna fish sandwiches." The four of them ate together—Mike had managed to make the dinner, simple as it was, feel like a special occasion—and afterward they got in the car to go shop at a mall. On the way Carolyn's breathing grew shallow and her heart beat faster. When she walked through the electric doors of the mall, the lights and movement and music and voices hit her with an unnatural and horrifying force. She fell to her knees and said, "Mike, I'm dying." He took her home and called her mother and said Carolyn was sick and asked if she would come and get the girls. Then he put Carolyn to bed. She spent the rest of the night cowering against the headboard. Mike sat at the foot of the bed, yelling. At times he knelt beside her, and at least once, he hit her. The LSD had been in her tuna fish. She felt better the next morning, but didn't recover for several days.

Carolyn left Mike and went back to him twenty times or more before she left him for good, in June of 1972. While Mike was in Michigan City, Carolyn had dated a man named Charlie. When it came time for Mike to get out, Carolyn told Charlie she thought it would be for the best if they didn't see each other anymore. One morning, Mike came home after being gone several days. Carolyn was in her robe, getting ready for work. The look that he gave her as he walked through the door was calmer and more deliberate than any he had given her before. He said, "I know about Charlie." She thought, If you don't leave, Carolyn, you are going to die. She turned away to compose herself, and when she turned back, she said, "I'm not feeling so well. I think I'll call my boss and say I'm not coming to work today."

Carolyn and Mike had no phone, so she went to her neighbor's. She called the man she worked for and told him she wouldn't be coming in anymore. Then she called her mother and described to her the place she wanted her to be waiting with the car. When she returned, Carolyn woke the girls and sent them to play in the yard. She told Mike that there was no bread for breakfast, and asked if he would get some. He nodded. Then he looked at her and said, "I love you," and she said, "I love you." Then she said she thought she would do a few loads of laundry. She went around the house with two laundry baskets, one for her and one for the girls, collecting clothes. She filled each basket with clean clothes and put dirty clothes on top. She went downstairs and left the baskets by the door. At the bottom of the stairs was a bathroom where Carolyn kept a set of electric curlers. They were the only gift she could recall Mike's ever buying for her, and when she went out the door, a few minutes later, she took them.

Mike left to get the bread. Carolyn waited until his car turned the corner, then gathered the girls and left the laundry and the curlers with the neighbor and struck out across a field in the direction opposite to the one Mike had taken.

She crossed a highway and met her mother, who drove them away and later went back for the clothes. That evening her mother and stepfather drove her and the girls to the bus station in Louisville, and they boarded a bus for Bowling Green, Kentucky, where her father lived. They stayed six years. She never answered any of the dozens of letters Mike sent through her mother for fear of his finding her. She feels that leaving Mike and staying away was the bravest thing she ever did in her life.

WHEN CAROLYN WENT OUT THE DOOR of the apartment she left it ajar, so Mike probably knew when he got back that something had happened. He told a friend that the first he knew for sure she was gone was when he walked through the door and saw the curlers were missing.

Mike spent a few minutes cursing and then he went to make some phone calls to see if he could turn up any hint of where she was. People in the apartment complex told Carolyn that in the days after she left they saw Mike in the yard with a hose filling the wading pool that the girls had played in. He went to see Carolyn's mother with a pair of their baby shoes, but she was unwilling to help him. Over the years, Mike grew obsessed with finding Carolyn and often showed up at her mother's and pleaded for information. He said that he still loved Carolyn and wanted to put his family back together and that he was no longer the person he'd been. Carolyn's mother thought that once you'd seen how he was capable of acting, it wasn't worth the risk to believe he had changed.

Mike paid no rent on the apartment. He sold what he could of the furniture, and what was left the apartment owner took to satisfy the debt, so Carolyn lost everything. Not long after she'd gone, Mike was picked up for passing checks he had stolen. The police must have been waiting for him because they arrested him right outside the apartment. No sirens, and Mike would never have let them follow him home if he'd seen them.

SOME OF THE TIME when Carolyn hadn't known where Mike was, he was holding up businesses or robbing people or breaking into their houses and stealing their possessions and selling them later for what he could get. One evening he stopped at a filling station and shut the old man working there in a back room, and said that if he came out he would kill him. He pumped gas for several customers and took their money, then pulled his car into the bay and filled the backseat and the trunk with tires and the tire changer and some tools and took off. He picked on filling stations often because they were simple: go in and get your money and back out the door, so no one can reach for a gun. Another night he was riding around Indianapolis with a friend when he pulled up in front of an apartment building and said he had to see a man inside, then came back carrying a television. The friend says you never could tell when Mike would do something like that, and the annoying thing about it was that it involved you in the crime. Occasionally he'd steal outboard motors from boats parked in driveways. One time he and a friend stole a canoe from Sears by carrying it out the door, as if they had paid for it.

Mike didn't usually own a gun, but he had carried a knife for as long as anyone who knew him could remember. As a boy he had been tormented by a bully until he stabbed the bully in the arm. People familiar with Mike knew that violence was part of his character. Something was necessary to set him off, but no one ever knew what might do it. One night he was at a chicken stand on Shelby Avenue when a dispute with another customer over something trivial expanded until the guy said, "You better back off, because I know karate," and Mike said, "Oh, yeah?" and put his cigarette out in the man's eye, then beat him nearly senseless. Mike would occasionally try to intimidate people, but he was not physically formidable. He unnerved others more often by the strangeness and abruptness of his behavior than by the suggestion of physical threat. Also, he had that prison habit of getting in the first strike and then disappearing. People who knew him feared him more when they couldn't see him, or when he was behind their backs.

It was always possible to tell when Mike had made money, because he was excessively fond of clothes. He liked black leather coats and expensive shoes. Whatever he wore had to have a brand name to it. Among the people he travelled with the thing to do was to find yourself in a situation where you could kick off your shoes and display the label inside. One of Mike's favorite shoes was a pair of patent-leather pumps. He and his friends dressed in imitation of the slicker black men they knew and saw around the city. He had a closetful of suits. He liked tight pants of an Italian cut and to go with them a kind of Italian knit shirt that had cloth-covered buttons. He also liked silk underwear, in colors to match his outfits. The hair on the back of his neck was cut to a sharp, straight line with a razor. He brushed his teeth three times a day, five minutes each time to a clock. He took oatmeal baths for his skin and used fragrant lotions to preserve it. He polished his fingernails with toothpaste. In photographs he appears to be a soft, fleshy young man, trim by the standards of the sixties, with fair skin, soft hands, clearly interested in matters of dress, and experimenting with styles of clipped beards. To younger men he was often a figure of some glamour.

He spent his nights charming housewives and office girls in nightclubs. While they drank cocktails in the dark and threw their heads back and laughed, Mike reached into their purses. When he found a wallet, he excused himself and took it to the bathroom and removed the credit cards or the checkbook and left the cash and returned to the table and sneaked the wallet back into the bag. By the time the women discovered their cards were missing, he'd signed their names all around town. Their checks he made out to himself, in order to cash them with his own identification.

If Mike could help it, he wouldn't go without money or drugs. Sometimes he would insert himself as a middleman into a drug transaction, and other times he would buy drugs for someone who didn't know where to get what he wanted, and the arrangement would be that the customer would buy something for Mike. He would tell doctors that he was staying at a hotel and that among the soap and shampoo the maid had swept off the top of the bureau was his prescription for depression. Or he'd say that he'd just passed a kidney stone. What story he used depended on the drug he desired. He could persuade people of anything, but the real reason he was convincing was that he presented the appearance of a truthful person. "He looked like butter wouldn't melt in his mouth," people say about him. Or, "He looked like a choirboy."

"He would be all right if you started out with him," says a man who knew him. "But if you only had an acquaintance with him—look out. He'd use your name, or steal your credit cards or your license any time he just needed an identity. When you first met him, you couldn't help but like him—he was well dressed and he made you laugh—but that could wear thin once you saw how he did."

In the beginning of the seventies, Mike fell in with a crowd that carried on a night life in the clubs around Indianapolis, and that was how he met Lee Von Hauger. Von Hauger is now in his early fifties. Everyone who knows him calls him Skip. He is about five foot ten, with a barrel chest, and shoulders wide enough to fill a doorway. He has blond hair with a tight curl and a blond beard. His face is round. His eyes are small and blue and watchful. His manner is cheerful and welcoming, and not without charm, but it can suddenly become distant and suspicious and imposing. He does calisthenics every morning in front of the television, following the lead of a man and a woman exercising on a beach in Hawaii. Much of his time he spends seated at his kitchen table, beside a speakerphone mounted on the wall. A number of years ago he began buying old houses and fixing them up. He engaged ex-convicts and homeless people for help, and when the work was completed he would let them live in the houses as tenants. Skip has a raspy, booming voice that is theatrical in its textures. It can modulate from calm to menace in a word. A way to witness this transformation is to be present when a tenant calls and says he will not be able to meet his month's rent.

Skip and his friends used to gather in the evenings at a club called Rat Finks and one night someone brought Mike around. Skip's impression of Mike was that he was a "normal, banal guy, with the middle-class life, the apartment and the two-point-two kids." He thought also, though, that Mike had a rebellious side he had never really known what to do with, and that when he fell in with Skip and his friends it was as if he had found himself.

"I had a whorehouse," Skip says, "most of the time I had around six or seven girls working for me, but I got up to fourteen girls one time. We'd go out partying and what I'd be doing was looking for new whores, bring them back and sign them up, new members of the harem. And Mike would be a runner for me. Some girl needed pantyhose, or a ride to a trick, or had to put gas in the car, Mike would do that. I gave him money and fed him and gave him clothes. He and I were the same size—I was a speed freak then—so he could wear my clothes. He'd go home every once in a while and change. Carolyn would be there, mostly real mad. He OD'd one time and Carolyn called me up, and I went over with some speed and jump-started him."

Skip and his crew mostly wore suits stolen by thieves they called boosters, men who stole mainly high-class things. The boosters employed spotters—people who occupied the attention of the cashier or the salesperson while the boosters went to work—and Skip thinks Mike may have worked as a spotter. "Mainly in his off-time he was scuffling," Skip says. "You go out on the street and you see something or you talk to somebody, and they tell you about something happening and you check it out. I didn't have eyes on him all the time, so he could have been up to a lot of other stuff. But, like I say, mostly he was a punk for me. It was common for pimps to have someone looking over the girls, often a gay man, and the joke was, when they were having trouble with the punk, 'Don't make me call the agency and get another punk.' "

"Mike and Skip were friends," says someone who knew them, "kind of, but when they got ten feet away from each other they'd talk about each other like dogs."

Part of Mike's reaction to Skip was based on envy, and part of Skip's to Mike was based on mistrust. Mike saw things in Skip's character that were absent from his own and that he desired. He modeled his appearance after Skip's. In Skip he saw someone older and smarter and more capable. Skip was a gangster, a man of some personal force in control of an outfit, and that was what Mike wished to be. Skip liked Mike, but also felt he was unreliable. Mike was pulled over once driving Skip's Cadillac. The cop who stopped him discovered that Mike had failed to answer a warrant. To stay out of further difficulty Mike offered to set up Skip on a drug deal. Skip came to suspect Mike had made an arrangement with the law. He fed Mike a quantity of psylicibin, then asked him some questions, and Mike gave up the plan.

Skip enlarged himself even further in Mike's eyes by getting Mike released from a state farm outside Indianapolis. He drove out to the farm in a white Cadillac with naked girls on the hubcaps and with the best-looking redhead he knew and placed a writ obtained from the court in the hands of the warden. "That sprung him," Skip says. "And it made an impression. That's the stuff legends are built up out of, and as I look back on it, it really caused my stock to soar with Mike." For years, when Mike found himself stranded in prison he would turn to Skip with an enormous hopefulness, then curse him for not being able to repeat the miracle.

IN 1972, Mike was given four years for passing bad checks and sent to the Indiana Reformatory in Pendleton, where Skip was already serving time for drug possession. Mike worked in the prison laundry and delivered Skip his sheets and clothes, carefully folded.

The years went by. Skip was released from Pendleton first. When Mike left, in March of 1976, he went to Florida to see a friend. His stepfather died in Mississippi while Mike was away and he missed the funeral. He went to his mother's house and got into an argument with one of his brothers and stabbed him. His family tried to have him confined in a hospital and treated for an addiction to heroin, but he went to Indianapolis and knocked at Skip's door and asked to be taken in.

Skip became interested in psychotherapy while in prison and when he got out he established a practice. His card described him as a "personal growth consultant." Mainly he was working with other ex-cons. They lived in his house and split chores and had sessions of group therapy. Mike moved in and Skip received money from Mike's mother to help pay the costs of keeping him.

Mike's stay in Pendleton had not been as rigorous as the time he had done in Michigan City, but still he felt unsettled by the stress and violence and restriction of prison. His behavior became peculiar. He began to stare. He would sit down opposite someone and stare at that person and lean over and strike a match on the floor then laugh in a way that struck others as hollow and hysterical.

When he wasn't staring at someone, his eyes raced around the room.

One night, while Skip was lying in bed with Cindy, his wife, Mike came running in. He was naked and he jumped up on the bed and danced around, and then he started laughing and ran from the room. Cindy stared at Skip. She had never seen Mike until then, and she decided he was disturbing and that she didn't like having him around.

Mike stayed, but he remained aloof from the life of the house. He wouldn't join the others at the table for meals. Instead, he would take his plate into the room beside the dining room and listen to the conversation coming to him through the doorway. From time to time, he would add something, but never loud enough for anyone to be certain of what he had said. Skip and Cindy felt that the remarks they heard from the room where Mike sat alone were words and phrases and sentences that Mike was hearing in his head and was saying out loud to see whether they provoked any reaction. Problems among members of the house were re-solved in sessions in which everyone took part—except Mike. He would attend, but if anyone raised an objection to his behavior he got up and left. Although everyone had responsibilities around the house, Mike would accept none.

One morning in June he pulled a toy gun on a woman who lived in the house and she went right for his throat. Skip stepped between them. In the scuffle Mike fell and Skip kicked him in the head. Then he threw Mike out the door and locked it. Mike stood in the driveway and shouted for someone to throw him his address book. No one did. He picked up a tree branch from the lawn and went along the side of the house breaking every window. The police found him standing in the front yard yelling at the house and arrested him for disorderly conduct. Skip told the police that lately Mike hardly slept and that he had stolen money from people in the house. In the hope of getting Mike off his hands, Skip jazzed up his grievances. He told the police that Mike had threatened to kill him and his wife and his children.

Because Mike had been behaving strangely, he was taken not to jail but to a hospital with a mental health clinic. The first doctor who examined him described him as weighing a hundred forty-two pounds. When the doctor asked Mike a question, Mike either shouted his answer or asked another question. He occasionally abandoned one subject for another that had nothing to do with the first. The doctor asked if Mike knew where he was and what time it was and the date and Mike said that he did. The doctor asked if he ever saw people or things that weren't actually there, or heard voices in his head, or believed emphatically in ideas he knew later not to be true, and Mike said he never had.

The days of the week passed. Mike's mother told a person who worked at the clinic that Mike sometimes spoke of his dreams as if they were things that really happened and that he had a laugh that "wasn't natural." Mike told one clinician after another that he had no problems, that he acted violently only when provoked, and that what set off his fit was that someone had stolen money from him. Mostly he would look the clinicians in the eye, but at times he would cut his eyes to the side and his voice would trail off until no one could make out what he was saying. Sometimes he wore sunglasses. He hated being kept in the hospital and felt stigmatized by being confined to the mental ward. He kept asking, "What do I have to do to get out of here?"

He told the therapists that he wanted to control the anger

he felt and cooperate, but the way he carried himself gave them the opposite impression. "People keep talking about the past," he said. "I've paid my dues being in prison for nine years. I don't know why they don't release me. Maybe I should keep my mouth shut and stay in a corner and they will release me." In asking to be transferred, Mike would insist that the only problems he had were ones that could not be solved while he was confined. What he needed, he said, was a job in construction, a woman who was sincerely concerned about his well-being, and a place in a school where he could study to be a beauty operator. A job where he could spend his time running his fingers through women's hair appealed to him.

Skip and a therapist told Mike that he was not taking responsibility for himself and was causing his own problems. Mike said that he felt he was being punished for no reason. Then he turned threatening. Skip told the therapist after the session that he was worried about Mike's threats and that Mike had shot a man with a shotgun by his house, although this hadn't happened; Skip was doing what he could to see that Mike remained where he was. He also said that Mike thought of himself as a hit man and that he would not hesitate to act on any delusions he entertained. The therapist made a note at the bottom of his report: "Sociopathic personality, paranoid with homicidal tendencies."

Mike's case was continued and he was let go free. Skip would not take him in, so he went to his mother's in Mississippi. Around the first of July he got into an argument with one of his brothers and was arrested. He sat in jail for three weeks. When he was offered a transfer to the State

Hospital, he accepted. He arrived there on July twenty-second, thirty years old. He took part in a process of talking and test-taking that was becoming familiar. To a doctor who asked about his background he said that he had started taking drugs when he was eighteen, and had been using heroin since getting out of prison four months before. He gave the doctor the impression that he was thinking carefully before speaking. The doctor wrote he suspected Mike to be "quite a sophisticated liar." As to the formalities of the interview, the doctor noted that he had been unable to discover in Mike ideas he considered paranoid or any that suggested Mike was suffering delusions. It had been suggested that Mike was afflicted with paranoid schizophrenia, but for that condition to be accurately diagnosed, a person must be suffering delusions or hallucinations; it is an aspect of the condition the diagnosis insists on. Mike's memory was intact, he knew where he was, the things that he said made sense; nothing about him seemed distorted.

The doctor wrote in his report, "Certainly it is evident from the patient's history that he is a grossly selfish, irresponsible, impulsive individual who is unable to feel guilt or learn from experience and punishment. Certainly his frustration tolerance is low." Mike's mother described ways Mike behaved that suggested he might be unbalanced, but the doctor felt it was difficult to tell whether drugs might not be responsible. He closed, "It is my opinion based on numerous interviews with this patient during, though brief, hospitalization, he demonstrated no psychotic or schizophrenic behavior." Antisocial personality was the diagnosis. Under "Prognosis" was the entry "Poor."

Mike left the hospital after five days. His commitment

had been voluntary, and the hospital could hold him no longer.

A YEAR PASSED. In September of 1977 Mike began studying at a beauty school in a Mississippi town near the Tennessee border. About two weeks later he found himself engaged in a familiar occupation: staring at the ceiling of a prison cell. This one in Nashville, the DeBerry Correctional Institute. Alone in his cell, he felt himself to be God. He heard movie stars, the President, his mother, his brothers, his sisters, and his daughters calling his name. He saw their faces and he saw the faces of people from other planets.

In the spring of 1978 he wrote,

Dearest Skip,

I understand why you didn't want to become involved in my life again. The way it was you had nothing to gain by it. I was still a taker. But all that's changed. Perhaps you're wondering how I can say that and be in prison on another charge. A rape charge. But I can say it knowing it to be the truth. First of all—I know why I did it. For one I thought I was having financial problems and I made myself think somehow that the only thing for me to do was rob and steal. Really confused. I got drunk, drove into a shopping center with intentions of robbing somebody, snatching a purse. Dumb, stupid shit. Damn. Skip, I wish I could turn time back and do it different. Knowing what I know now. But I can't. I got in a car with a woman. I was drunk as hell. Forced my way in the car to take the money, then she said, "I'll

give you what you want, just don't hurt me"—so I de-
cided to fuck too. Damn I was sick, Skip. I was more
afraid than she was and that's a fact. But I was wrong,
really wrong. I just really made a bad mistake. . . .
They offered me a 1–5 a year ago with a public de-
fender. I thought then that maybe I could do better with
a private attorney. So I paid $1,000.00 and ended up
with ten years. . . . So I'm through with that for now. I
just wanted you to know how and where I stand. I
want you to see it standing in my shoes. . . . But let's
find another basis for beginning again somewhere. Right
here. Eventually it will be legally profitable to you as
well as myself. If you want to do it. I'll explain that to
you later in detail. It's only a living working relation-
ship. I'm going to be a beautician and I'm going to be
good. Maybe you're wondering how you could fit into
that. But you can if you want to and it can be profita-
ble. But I'm moving too fast. . . . Forget that and re-
member our friendship for a minute. I guess you've been
an idealist father figure to me, Skip. I love my father
because he's my father. But I've never admired him. He
left when I was only 8 years old. He never helped me
out with anything. Only pretended to. As I used to do.
He never showed me how to do anything. Just nothing.
I haven't any pleasant memories with him. None at all.
But I still love him. He's my father. . . . But that's
enough about him. I'm going to be in the penitentiary
for another three years. . . . So where does that leave it.
I'm thinking about me and mine. . . . I'm learning. To
be a beautician that is—by the time I get back to you
I'll be a good one. I'll be a coiffeur—don't that sound

*good. But I miss you, Skip. . . . Can't wait to get back
to all of you. It's going to be right. Did you notice how
I had let myself go? Aside from living so many lies, I
was physically smashed too, Skip. I am 6 ft tall when I
stand straight. But I went down to 147 pounds. Slump
shouldered and even balding. Teeth bad too. And didn't
mind stealing folks shit. But forget that. And did you
know that washing your hair too often can make the
scalp dry, close the pores, cause dandruff, and can cause
alopecia, or baldness? And that had been my problem. I
washed my hair every time I took a shower—every day
—and it was drying my scalp, closing the pores, and
causing me to go bald— But I've long since stopped
washing the hair every day—I've taken treatments—oil
—and it may sound like crazy shit but believe it, it's
true. My hair is growing back thick again. I'm getting
myself together up there and I'm really working on my
appearance too. The physical things. I'm gaining good
pounds. The weights looking good on me. Correcting my
posture. Working on the legs. I'm having all the front
teeth removed. The colors bad—I'll have it bridged as
soon as I get out. I want to be rid of the 2 pds of metal
it takes to hold the partial in. Anyway, I'll have a nice
clean white mouth and that's what I want. To Skip.
Will you open your mouth real wide and smile real big
and have somebody take a close up of your teeth and
send me the picture? I'm going to try and have the
bridges made like yours with the gold in mine the way
yours used to be. If you don't mind. Just send me a good
picture. . . . I'm sending you one taken December 77.
. . . But this is the only one I've got right now. And I*

*can't have pictures taken now. I could—but I'm not
seeing as how I'm having operations. I've just yesterday
—Friday—had nose surgery—Opened sinus cavity's and
removed about 2 pounds bone and flesh. That should
leave the nose somewhat smaller. . . . But the operation
left my face swollen and bruised. My nose is braced and
bandaged. My eyes are black and my whole face swollen. I go back in three weeks for a face lift. Taking
some wrinkles out of my forehead and lifting the eye-
brows. Then after that I'm having another operation on
my hand. Then the only thing left to be done is the
bridged teeth. Of major appearance changes, that is, but,
Skip, I've revealed a great deal of myself to you. Nobody
has forced me to do it of course. I'm doing it because I
want to do it. Because my best memories unbelievably
were made after I met you, and you I feel are responsible for the biggest and best changes in my life, whether
you know it or not, in that I've admired you. I've
wanted to be like you and it's affected my life greatly. I
regret many things. I regret being so stupid. I regret that
it's taken so many years to make me see change, head it
in the right direction and put it in gear. So I've got this
one last pit stop before I can return to the city and be a
part of your life again. . . . And I need you. I need your
cards and letters. It doesn't take much to occasionally
tell me how you are doing. And would you no matter
how dumb the request. . . . So send some pictures, Skip
. . . and remember and have one taken of your teeth for
me. Skip—don't let me down. Write me—just a note—
a card—or have someone to do it for you. . . . I love
you, Skip. . . . I love you all very much. But I'm going*

*to begin and get this ready and in the mail. Write me. I
love you. And I miss you, Skip. Love.*

Mike.

Modean took Mike's daughters to the prison. This was
in November of 1979. The girls had been with her in Mississippi for the fall—they remember rolling hills and red
clay—and in taking them back to Indianapolis she stopped
at the prison without telling them where they were going.
They simply arrived. The girls sat on a couch in a room
with other inmates and their visitors. They posed for their
grandmother's camera. The younger girl, a blonde, leaned
toward her father. The other, dark-haired, stood apart. She
remembered very little having to do with her father, except
running through the fields from the house with her mother.
She says that she was a bitter child but that she didn't really
miss having a father because, never having had one, she
didn't know what there was to miss. She had no desire to
see him. Her sister and her grandmother talked often about
him, and her grandmother had given her sister pictures of
him. Mike told his daughters they had beautiful hair and
gave them advice on how to take care of it. They stayed an
hour. It was the first time they had seen him since they left
with their mother.

The next day Mike wrote to Carolyn: "It's incredible how
they've grown—they're very beautiful. I've missed so much.
I was so sorry a husband, never a father, nothing can express
the sorrow for not having taken hold—we could have grown
together happily, I'm sure."

Mike was released in August of 1982. His confinement
had been difficult. He was often withdrawn. At times he

seemed to slip into a psychotic state and was violent. He spent time in the psychiatric wing of the prison. He wrote threatening letters to several people, including his mother and Skip. Sometimes he wrote things on the envelopes he sent his mother which embarrassed her to the point where she explained the situation to her postman, so that he would draw no discreditable conclusions. Eventually Mike was placed on medication, which had to be forced on him, but as it began to work he accepted it. At the time he was under consideration for a bed at the state mental hospital but the medication improved him, and commitment was no longer thought necessary.

From prison Mike had often written to Carolyn. She had lived on the run for eight years. She married a man in Bowling Green, but the marriage didn't last. She married in the hope of finding security, but felt she picked the wrong person for that. When she moved back to Indianapolis, with a different last name, she called Modean, who was living in Mississippi, and asked, "Where's Mike?" She didn't want him returned to her life by accident. In prison, was Modean's answer. From time to time Carolyn called to learn whether there had been any change. She never let Modean know where she was living, or what her new name was.

FOR SEVERAL MONTHS after his release, Mike lived with his mother in Pontotoc, Mississippi. He enrolled in a beauty school, but quit because he found the reading required for the classes too hard. He took a part-time job as a maintenance worker at an apartment complex. He applied for a job at a factory making air compressors, but didn't get it. He bought a car. He called the state employment office in

Indianapolis and asked if they could find him a job. They told him that there weren't many jobs available, but that they might find something for him at a restaurant. He wrote Skip that he found living in Pontotoc "absolutely utterly dull and boring," and that if it weren't for the company of his mother, "I couldn't bear a minute here."

He made visits to a doctor in Tupelo. He felt nervous and depressed and his head ached. Sometimes he was nauseated and threw up. One of the doctors who saw him for the purpose of determining whether he was eligible for disability payments for emotional reasons observed that Mike paced the floor and that his manner was blunt and without emotion. The doctor noted on the form sent by social security that Mike gave no evidence of psychosis, but that his activities were severely restricted and that he was unable to handle money.

Four months later, he was back in the Mississippi State Hospital, committed by his mother. She told doctors he was in the habit of lying on the couch in the living room without any clothes on and walking around the house naked too. She found a pornographic magazine among his possessions. Sometimes he would start singing. Now and then, what he said seemed intended for the ears of people who weren't in the room. Late at night he would wake his mother by turning his radio up loud. When she came to see what the noise was, she found him with the radio against his ear. He went around the house turning mice out of traps she put down. He was supposed to be visiting the local mental health clinic, but he kept missing appointments and refusing the medication the clinic prescribed. The charge on which his mother had him arrested was lunacy.

To a doctor, he said that the problem was his mother's. He said he had walked through the house without any clothes, but had been drinking bourbon at the time and had taken his clothes off to get into the shower. He wanted out of the hospital and to attend hotel and motel management school in Indianapolis. He felt nothing was wrong with him. He used to be exciting when he was young, he said, and wanted to be so again.

While Mike was in the State Hospital, he was tested to determine his intelligence; he was asked to look at inkblots and say what they put him in mind of, he was asked to complete sentences, and he was asked questions to which he was to answer true or false. He took part reluctantly.

The intelligence test established his IQ at about ninety-nine, or average. He scored so poorly on one part of the test that the clinician analyzing the results concluded that he may have been depressed. Perhaps Mike was capable of a higher score, he said, but even so it was likely to remain average.

His impressions of the inkblots were familiar to the clinician as the response of "people who are paranoid and who (1) are not sure just what the consequences of their responses will be, and (2) don't want to be held accountable for what they said." The clinician went on to report that Mike saw little around him as "attractive and positive"; mostly he saw things as "ugly"; he was oversensitive, and led a life that was emotionally barren and involved little interest in the lives of other people.

"I am?" he was asked.

"A man," he replied.

"It is wrong?"

"To do wrong."
"I look upon myself as?"
"Peaceful."
To the following statements:

Once in a while I think of things too bad to talk about.
At times I feel like swearing.
I do not always tell the truth.
Once in a while I put off until tomorrow what I ought
to do today.
My table manners are not quite as good at home as
when I am out in company.
I like to know some important people because it makes
me feel important.
Sometimes at elections I vote for men about whom I
know very little.
Once in a while I laugh at a dirty joke.

he answered "False."
Someone whose answers fit the pattern Mike's did is not
likely, in the clinician's opinion, to be able to endure frustration. He is likely to harbor anger and resentment which
are intense and might turn him toward violence as a means
of slaking them. He is likely to have trouble occupying the
sexual role of a man. He is also likely to have few resources
for tolerating demands made by women. Mike drew the
attention of the clinician by answering "True" to the state-
ment "I am strongly attracted by members of my own sex"
and then retracting his answer, saying that he didn't want
anyone to think he was "queer."
Mike left the hospital on the tenth of March after staying

a month. He was picked up by one of his brothers and went back to live with his mother.

FOR THE NEXT YEAR, he went back and forth between Mississippi and Indiana. He had headaches and trouble sleeping. He gained fifty pounds in six months. He had his hair permed. He worked in a Waffle House but quit because he couldn't remember orders. He lived in a house of Skip's in a run-down part of the city. A sixteen-year-old girl named Phyllis Wright was living there with her mother and with two of her four brothers when Mike arrived with a friend.

"They drove up in this old blue car," says Phyllis, "and you could see through the hatchback that everything they owned in the world was in there, bags and clothes, and things all piled in, and Mike looked like some kind of transient. They came up the walk and said, 'Can we see the place?' and I didn't know what they were there for, and I said, 'Well, why?' and they said, 'Well, Skip said we could live here.'"

Phyllis didn't at all like the way Mike looked. She called Skip and gave him hell, but he wanted more money from the house. She and her mother and her brothers moved out. Mike became friends with one of her brothers—Travis, who was seventeen. Travis and Mike drove to Pontotoc to visit Mike's mother. Travis thought a person under eighteen was allowed to cross state lines only in the company of his parents, so he carried with him a note from his mother. While Mike and Travis were driving around in Mike's old VW, Mike saw a pickup for sale on a secondhand lot.

"Mike just fell in love with it," Travis says. "He went home and told his mom, and she had a new VW van, and a couple of days later she had talked to the man at the lot and had a deal where she gave him her new van and some money and got the truck, and she got Mike's old car, so she didn't come out too good on the deal."

Down a dirt road through woods in the country outside Indianapolis Mike and Travis found a camper top someone had pitched down a stream bank. It was too long for the bed of Mike's truck but he took a hacksaw to it, then painted it black. It never fit exactly right, but he liked it. The truck had shiny mag wheels and a black interior, no rust or dents, and was painted a light shade of blue. A photograph in his mother's possession, taken in November of 1983, shows Mike standing before the truck in the yard of her house in Mississippi. His arms are folded across his chest and he is leaning against the truck. The pose is self-conscious and formal and suggestive of simple, deep pride of ownership.

IN DECEMBER OF 1983 Mike sent Carolyn three poems. One he called "Sleep Warm" began, "I sleep soundly, I sleep softly, knowing you sleep warm." Another called "Just Passing Through Again!!" began:

> *We pass the signs*
> *The seasons*
> *and the signposts now*
> *at such a speed*
> *That pausing to reflect*
> *on what direction means*
> *grows harder year by year*
> *and yet your God and mine*
> *daily holds his breath*

*expecting us to listen
and to care about each other.*

The third he called "Sometimes I Want To Be A Little Girl."

*Sometimes I want to be a little girl—
To hear stories of princes
    Kissing sleeping maidens
And castles towering high on mountains
    Where elegant men
Waltz with willowy ladies
    To soft violins
As the stars blink their eyes
    In the glow of the moon.*

*Sometimes I want to be a little girl—
To eat popcorn and animal crackers
    And soft, sugary fudge;
To giggle behind closed doors
    At guessing games and secrets;
To wear floppy slippers and chew my pigtails
At ghosts & witches wandering in the night—
Cuddling beneath a howling wind and the rain on the roof.*

*Sometimes I want to be a little girl—
    So touch my cheeks lightly
    Play with my hair
        Stroke me
            Without passion or grasping
            Without expectations*

In feather beds and gentleness—
Because—I am a little girl.

Carolyn was not sure if he'd written the poems or not. She tried to find out if anyone had ever heard them before and no one told her that he had, and she found them in no book.

FOR A FEW WEEKS in 1984 Mike studied welding at a junior college in Tupelo. He earned several A's and one B and then gave it up. "He never wanted to finish anything," says his mother. "He always just quit." In March, he hit one of his brothers on the head with an iron and threatened his mother and ended up in the state hospital again. To yet another doctor, he said nothing was wrong with him, that if people would leave him alone he would be all right, and that any difficulties his mother reports having with him were her fault, not his.

The doctors prescribed drugs which appeared to calm him. He got along with the other patients but kept to himself. He was confined to the grounds for two months. In the middle of May he went home on a pass and lived with his mother for two weeks without friction. The doctors decided he could be discharged. He went to live with his mother again.

A YEAR WENT BY. One day in February of 1985 Mike went into a hardware store outside Tupelo and bought some galvanized pipe. To be certain he had the proper diameter he brought with him a twelve-gauge shotgun shell. When he found the size that accepted the shell he bought three pieces, the longest of which was eighteen inches. He paid about five dollars for the pipe and a bolt. Then he drove out Highway 6 from Pontotoc until he reached open fields. He inserted the shotgun shell in one end of the longest piece of pipe, and screwed a coupling behind it. Then he threaded a short piece of pipe into the coupling. With the palm of his hand he forced the point of the bolt into the cap of the shell, and felt the plumbing pipe jump in his hands. He had never made a shotgun before; in prison, he learned how.

One Tuesday night a few weeks later Mike broke several of his mother's ribs in a bear hug. The phone rang just after he released her. He was wearing slippers and pajamas and a bathrobe, and the ringing startled him. He grabbed a coat that belonged to his brother and some boots and ran to his truck. His departure was so abrupt he left his dental plate behind.

He drove that night up Route 55, through Memphis, and slept by the road, went on through Arkansas and Missouri, then turned east and by Thursday he was in Indianapolis. He went to see one of his sisters, who worked in a store selling health foods and vitamins and nutritional supplements. She hadn't laid eyes on Mike for a year. She heard from her sister what happened to their mother, and was upset about it. He asked for money and she refused him. He started to curse her and she told him to leave the store, that if he didn't she would call the police. Mike said, "You won't be able to do it much longer," which she took as a threat. He drove out into the country. Around one-thirty in the afternoon one of his brothers, who was living in a town near Indianapolis, saw Mike in his truck in front of his house. When the brother opened his door, Mike took off. He drove past Skip's house several times. In the yard of a hospital he picked up some syringes he found on the ground and put them in his pocket. Somewhere he bought four large plastic soda bottles and cut the tops off. He filled a five-gallon can in the bed of his truck with a mixture of gasoline and diesel fuel. The mixture he poured into the bottles and then he found some cloth, which he cut into four strips. One end of each of the strips he stuck into the bottles. He planned to spend the night at the Lighthouse Mission of the Salvation Army, but didn't have the money, so he slept in his truck. At ten-thirty the next morning he went to a market, made three salads at the salad bar, took them to the register, had them weighed and priced ($1.99), and walked out the door. The security guard working for the market stopped him in the parking lot. He brought Mike into the market's office and in the pockets of his pants and coat found five shotgun shells, fifteen twenty-two-caliber cartridges, three pocketknives, and five or six syringes. The guard called the Indianapolis police, who found in their records a warrant for Mike issued two years earlier for driving while drunk. When the police asked Mike for his address, he gave Skip's.

Before the police took him to jail they asked Mike if he had a car in the parking lot, and he said he didn't. One of the policemen noticed the truck and the Mississippi plates and asked his dispatcher to retrieve the name of the owner. He did not immediately know what to make of the pieces of galvanized pipe he found in the cab, but he figured it out pretty fast. What the Molotov cocktails were he knew right away.

Mike said he made the shotgun to protect himself against Skip, who had told him never to come back to Indianapolis and that he would shoot his face off the first time he saw him. The F.B.I. concluded that Mike had intended to use the firebombs to burn down the house of one of his sisters. Skip heard that Mike meant to set his house on fire and use the shotgun to shoot him as he ran from the flames.

Mike was held for trial at the Marion County Jail. Within a few weeks the head of the jail was familiar with the large, looping characters of Modean's writing. What she hoped to find was a place where Mike could be cared for as someone who was mentally ill. She said that she loved her son and stood with him and would do anything she could to help him.

Mike was sent for observation to the U.S. Medical Center for Federal Prisoners in Springfield, Missouri, so it could be determined whether he was competent to stand trial. On a form he filled out when he arrived, he answered the question, "In your own words, describe what happened before your current arrest," by writing, "Just built a gun to hunt and protect myself."

He told a room of clinicians that he was not an alcoholic, but that he drank all he could get and how much that was depended on his mood and the money he had. He said that he had done all the drugs there were. While he talked, he looked from one corner of the room to the other. Occasionally he laughed for no reason that anyone else could tell. Probably the questions he'd most frequently been asked since he'd turned twenty-one were did he hear any voices in his head and did he see any people or scenes he knew were not real, and when the staff asked them now he said he did not. He said that he was not mentally ill and never had been. When one of the clinicians told Mike he seemed depressed,

Mike said, "You just have to accept the way things are."

Mike told a doctor he had been arrested for everything except murder. He said he'd taken medications most of the last four and a half years but they only made him suffer.

The doctor wrote, "The patient has a full beard, a very hostile appearing attitude with a lot of underlying hostility, and appears to be a person who could quickly become aggressive."

THE SMALL DETAILS of life in prison. He was kept under close watch. He was heard bragging that he was "a real tough guy." He let his appearance slide and he began to smell. He pestered other inmates for stamps. Early one morning he seemed to be talking to three different people in his empty cell. On another occasion he was seen to be laughing. Sometimes he didn't leave his cell for days. He began to hoard food and magazines and newspapers and anything else he got his hands on. He complained that his shoes hurt and asked for new ones. He engaged in arguments. Other inmates accused him of stealing cigarettes. He stayed up all one night talking to himself and wouldn't let the light be turned off in his cell. For the rest of the day people had to yell to get his attention. After about a week and a half the food he hoarded had spoiled, and he was taken from his cell, which upset him. He threatened a guard and was lashed to his bed and spent a lot of time cursing. A few days later he apologized. Another guard observed him listening to a radio through headphones and talking. He asked Mike what he was doing and Mike said, "I'm talking to myself. I do that sometimes."

Not long after Mike arrived at Springfield, an official of the prison received a letter from a U.S. Attorney in Indianapolis saying that investigations by the Bureau of Alcohol, Tobacco, and Firearms revealed that Mike's family was "terrified of him."

The doctors at Springfield decided that Mike was fit to stand trial and sent him back to Indianapolis.

MIKE'S LAWYER, appointed by the court, advised him to plead insanity to the firearms charge. Mike objected to being described as crazy and asked the judge to dismiss the attorney. He said it was like having two prosecutors.

At his trial he said that he had come back to Indianapolis to be near his daughters and to try and work things out among them. He petitioned the court to command the phone company and the gas company to give him Carolyn's address and phone number so that she could appear on his behalf. Eventually he pleaded guilty. The Assistant U.S. Attorney who prosecuted him said that Mike at his sentencing had told him over and over, in a voice pitched low enough that the judge couldn't hear, "I'm going to kill you. I'm going to come back and kill you."

An inmate at the jail heard some things Mike said and knew whom he was referring to. The inmate wrote,

Skip
   Just thought I'd drop ya a line to let you know what's up. . . . this Mike Jackson fella is definitly loosely wraped. he's really talkin Crazy About you, so just watch your back. . . .

Mike was returned to Springfield to serve a sentence of a year for illegally having a gun. For the Molotov cocktails he was given three years of probation, to begin when he was released.

MIKE PASSED his year in confinement the way he passed most of his others: he lost control a few times and was punished; he answered questions from doctors and clinicians on matters such as how he was feeling and what he was thinking; he took tests intended to reveal aspects of his character; he played card games with other inmates; he was chatty at times, reclusive and withdrawn at others; he asked to be freed; he spent a certain amount of time in solitary confinement; he was sometimes interested in his appearance and sometimes not; sometimes kept his cell clean and ordered and sometimes did not. Mainly he lay on his back and stared at the walls and ceiling, or slept, or sat up and put his feet on the floor and leaned his elbows on his knees and put his head in his hands.

For a time he attended sessions of music therapy. He decided he wanted to play the drums. The therapist noted in her records that he took part in singing and discussion, or that he sang and tried to learn the fingerings of chords on the guitar, or, during a period of depression, that he looked mostly at the floor but took part in the singing. More than once she noted his desire to stay in music therapy all day.

His spirits rose and fell. Sometimes he refused to leave his bed or look at someone who spoke to him. He denied hearing voices or seeing visions but the way he laughed sometimes, when people least expected it, made the staff of the prison think he did. He let his beard and his hair grow long. His beard was thick and dark and crept toward the top of his cheeks. His face appeared mournful and haunted and maniacal. His eyes seemed to look into the distance.

WHILE MIKE WORKED off the days of his sentence the officials of the prison tried to think what to do with him once he was free. He was to be released in the middle of February, 1986. Modean had been writing the warden that Mike was dangerous and asking that he be kept in confinement. In December the warden wrote the director of social services in Indianapolis and asked if Mike could be placed in a state mental hospital. The reply was that only a court could decide so; given his past, it was unlikely a hospital would consider him capable of a voluntary commitment.

Later that month Mike appeared before a panel in the prison assembled to assess his condition. Its members decided he was suffering from "a significant mental disease or defect" and was "dangerous to others." They recommended that a place be found for him that was safe and structured and where he could be watched. Early in January Mike was given a new medication, called Mellaril. He shaved his beard and cut his hair. His thinking, which had struck the prison staff as being in disarray, seemed to become ordered. He talked slowly and had less difficulty remembering things. He spoke politely and stopped complaining and ingratiated himself with the staff and other inmates. He no longer told people he would kill them. He no longer seemed violent. During this period the panel met again and decided Mike could be released safely as long as he was taking his medication.

Early in February, the warden wrote Michael Trent, a

psychiatric social worker in Indianapolis who had agreed to counsel Mike. What the warden hoped was that Mike could be given his medicine at the Midtown Mental Health Clinic, where Trent worked, and have his mouth inspected to make sure he swallowed it. If he failed to show up for an appointment or refused the medicine or to have his mouth checked, someone would notify the court, and a warrant would be issued to return him to Springfield.

MIKE PASSED in a car through the gates of Springfield at twenty-five after five on the morning of April fourteenth. He was accompanied by a man from the staff of the prison, who took him to the airport, where they boarded a plane for St. Louis, then changed for Indianapolis, where they arrived at ten of eleven. From the airport they went to see Mike Trent.

Trent gave Mike his medication. Mike said he didn't like taking it—the medication made him sleepy—but he realized he must. Mike struck Trent as eager to find a place to live and a job. While he was in prison his driver's license expired, so he said he would depend on the buses in the city. As he talked to Trent the pitch of his voice hardly varied, his face showed little change of expression, and most of the time he sat still in his chair, conditions psychiatrists refer to as representing a flat or blunted affect, but Trent thought they might also be a result of the medication. His conversation rambled at times but he did not impress Trent as psychotic. They made an appointment to meet the next day.

Mike left with the man from the prison, who caught a plane back to Missouri. That night Mike called his mother from a pay phone on the street. He said he had the clothes he was wearing and forty-five dollars in his pocket. What he didn't have was anywhere to go.

THE NEXT DAY Mike told Trent that he had been refused a bed the night before by the Volunteers of America. This confused Trent, because he was led to believe by the officials at Springfield that they had arranged for Mike to stay there. When Trent called the Volunteers he learned that Springfield tried five times to reserve a place for Mike but was turned down because of his violent nature. Each time the prison officials observed an improvement in him they tried again. Mike was referred to the Lighthouse Mission, but decided he would rather stay at a place called Harbor Light, also run by the Salvation Army.

Over the next few weeks Mike met nearly every day with Trent. Modean mailed him money. He bought clothes at thrift stores. Trent gave him bus tickets. He asked Trent if it would be all right for him to drink.

At the end of the month Mike was referred to an agency that ran a program designed to help people whose condition made it difficult to hold a job. He was instructed to begin the way everyone else did, by carrying out chores around the premises, but he didn't like it.

He said that the medication made him drowsy and stupid. He didn't care for living at Harbor Light. He didn't want to push a broom around the halls of somebody's office for nothing as a means of developing useful habits; he wanted his mother to support him; he wanted a bug-free apartment for close to nothing; he wanted to see Carolyn; and he wanted to be involved in big-time, fast-buck, money-making ventures with friends. At some point it was borne in on

Trent that Mike never talked about the past, he only complained about the present.

He began selling blood twice a week. When they asked at the blood bank if he took medication, he said that he didn't.

Among his most ardent obsessions was recovering his truck. The truck had been parked at his brother's while Mike was in prison and the plates had expired. Also, it needed work. Modean wouldn't send him the title, so he couldn't get new plates, and he didn't have money to repair it.

He found work washing dishes in the kitchen of an expensive hotel, but quit in tears the first day. Too much pressure, he told Trent, and "too many people."

"When he got out of Springfield, they gave him his medication, and turned him loose, and he showed up at my door," says Skip. "The bastards never even let me know he was out." There was no question of Mike's living at Skip's—Skip would not tolerate that—but Mike began to appear at the kitchen door more and more frequently, always unannounced. Skip and Cindy noticed that Mike's speech had slowed, from the medication they guessed, into a kind of drawl. He whined about how his mother wouldn't send him the title to his truck, how he couldn't find work, and his ugly little room down at Harbor Light. Skip and Cindy were sympathetic, "because we liked him," says Cindy, and he was polite, but he also tried their patience. His walk had become awkward, as if he couldn't pick up his feet, a little thing they called the Thorazine shuffle.

He complained to Trent that his family was holding him back, particularly his mother by refusing him the title to his truck. He said he wanted nothing more to do with his family and would stop taking their money in exchange for the title. It was Trent's opinion that Mike depended too heavily on his mother and that he might do better on his own. Trent told Mike he would need his court order revised to include the agreement that he would not harass his family for money. Trent spoke to Modean, and she said that she would give Mike's title to his brother who already had the truck.

Mike then asked to have his medication discontinued, a consideration it was not in Trent's power to grant.

Mike finally turned the key on his truck. Trent had not had the court order revised, so Mike was violating nothing other than the spirit of the agreement when he asked his mother for money for new license plates. She wouldn't give it to him. "Someone should hang the bitch by her toes until she's dead," he told a friend. Then he and another friend drove to a junkyard where the wrecks still had their plates. While Mike went into the office and engaged the employees, his friend went out to the yard and removed an Indiana plate from the back bumper of one of the wrecks.

''THE FIRST TIME I saw him after he got out of Springfield I remember it was summer and I was sunbathing in my backyard and I didn't hear him come up." This is Phyllis Wright, the young woman who moved with her mother out of the house Skip owned when Skip moved Mike in. "He put his face down right over me, and said, 'Boo!' and when I opened my eyes he was just right there, and it really spooked me. I pulled my towel over me and got up."

Around the end of June, Phyllis and her mother and Travis agreed to let Mike use their bathroom and take meals with them and generally have the run of their house during the day, but Phyllis drew the line at his sleeping under their roof. She offered instead a place in their driveway for his truck, which had a mattress in the camper. Travis wanted to give him a key so that he could use the bathroom at night, but Phyllis said she didn't want Mike around when she was asleep. She didn't know Mike had served time as a rapist; he simply made her uneasy. To Travis and Mike she said that if Mike wanted to use the bathroom in the middle of the night, he could knock loud enough on the door to be heard. Mike said, "Phyllis, don't you trust me?" and she said that she didn't, and he just rolled his eyes and walked off.

Travis and Mike were in the habit of going out drinking in the evening. When they returned Phyllis was usually in bed. If she wasn't, Travis would wait until she retired, then let Mike in. He would spend the night in a sleeping bag on the floor of a room by the kitchen and let himself out before she got up.

Phyllis liked Mike during daylight just fine. He was helpful around the house, and at least while he was taking the medication his nature was "sweet." Phyllis and her mother had no car. Mike would drive them to the market or the movies and several times he took her mother to see relatives in the country. If her mother offered money for gas he wouldn't take it. "Day may come when I'll need it, and you can do it for me then," he would say.

The flatness of his expression they got used to, but Phyllis says that they found it "eerie." He reminded people on occasion of the characters on a cornflakes box. Sometimes it was as if he were wearing a mask. They never met Modean, but as they sat several months later in front of their television listening to her plead with Mike to turn himself in, the same thought went through both of their minds: that's just how Mike acted. Sometimes if he said something he thought was funny his face would go from no expression to registering a little laugh then return to no expression. Whatever Mike said—the simplest thing, or a thought of some complexity —seemed to take twenty minutes to explain. Even the most straightforward thought turned corners in his mind. To demonstrate how the drugs made him feel Mike would pull on his jaw. He would say that they slowed his thinking so much that he was never sure if he was saying what he meant to. He rarely raised his voice. He shouted only when drunk, or beside himself with anger.

TRENT AND A PSYCHIATRIST at the clinic wrote the court asking that Mike's conditions of release be amended so that he no longer be required to submit to a mouth check. He was about to begin a job-training program, they said, and could not take part if he was required to be at the hospital every morning.

That same day Mike told Trent he was roofing for a contractor and living in the contractor's house, which had no phone. The address he gave was Phyllis's.

The truth was Mike worked for Phyllis's mother, who supervised a crew that cleaned schools and factories at night. He was assigned to dustmop floors and carry out trash. He had trouble keeping up. "He couldn't understand things," says Phyllis's mother. "To tell him how to do something, you'd have to explain it two or three times. Then he wouldn't really get it right, and would get upset at himself for it. It was like he was simpleminded, or maybe it was the medication. The faster he moved, the slower he got."

He quit in tears soon after he started, and Phyllis's mother talked him into coming back. She said that the boss liked the job he was doing and that the crew was shorthanded and needed him.

MIKE CONSIDERED robbing a restaurant in a shopping mall. He was angry at a woman who worked at the restaurant. He wanted to rob the place while she was there and, according to Travis, "do something to her at the same time." He and Travis drove out one afternoon to look at the place, then stopped off at an apartment building, where, Travis says, "Maybe he had something going on, but he didn't tell me what." After they left the apartment they drove around the suburbs for a few hours drinking beer. Then they saw a car ahead of them weaving. Mike blew the horn and Travis leaned out the window and waved his arms, and they flagged it into the parking lot of a gas station. Mike asked the guys in the car if they knew where he could get any pot, and they said that they didn't but they had some LSD. Mike bought four hits and took two and Travis took two and they drove around about an hour more drinking beer, then came back into town and stayed up talking the rest of the warm summer night.

From time to time Mike would get in his truck and drive out into the country and knock at a preacher's door and say that he had no money and needed help to get on his feet. He'd also make the rounds of churches in the city that were giving away food. He'd return to Phyllis's house with two or three bags of groceries out of which he would separate what he wanted. The rest he would give to Phyllis and Travis and their mother as his contribution to the budget of the house.

Travis enjoyed Mike's company. If Mike had money he shared it, and he was always willing to start up his truck and take a drive and see what might turn up. The only time Travis felt nervous around Mike was when he drank too much. He lost his temper easily then and turned mean. He would get a few beers in him and start talking about his ex-wife and how she had influenced his daughters against him and what he would do to her if he ever tracked her down.

One night he said to Phyllis's boyfriend, "You let me know if anyone's bothering you, because if there is, I'll have to kill him."

"He didn't do stickups anymore," says Phyllis. "He was trying to hold jobs, but really he was trying to get disability. He would work a little, but mainly he held the attitude of why should I work for three dollars an hour when I can get money for nothing?"

In the first envelope from Social Security to arrive for Mike in Phyllis's mailbox were several checks. After picking them up, Mike was gone from the house the rest of the day. That night he told Phyllis a guy beat him up in a bar and stole his money, and he wondered what he would live on until the next check arrived. He was laughing ("You know how something bad can happen," Phyllis says, "and seem funny later"), but even so she didn't know whether to believe him, because he owed her money.

Mike worked satisfactorily for about two weeks on Phyllis's mother's crew. Then he started coming to her with complaints. He would say that Travis was upstairs reading instead of cleaning the room he'd been assigned, or that other members of the crew were talking instead of carrying out their tasks. He started threatening people he worked with, and the women, especially, grew afraid of him. They told Phyllis's mother that if she didn't run him off they were quitting. When she told him he was fired, he said he was going to come back and rip out her heart and shove it down her throat. A security guard saw him off the premises.

On July 30, Mike told Trent he had been promoted to supervisor of his housekeeping crew and given a raise. He mentioned that he hoped to buy a house.

He was still living with Phyllis and her mother and Travis. A few days after he lost the job, he came into the kitchen and started in with Phyllis about her mother. Phyllis got so angry in the argument that followed that tears came to her eyes. Travis was standing between her and Mike. When he moved aside, Phyllis pushed Mike backward out the door and locked it. He banged on the door for a while and then he went and sat in his truck. An hour passed. Phyllis went out and said, "You can't stay here anymore, Mike. You have to leave."

Mike happened to know that Phyllis's mother was shopping at a drugstore. He found her in line, and started yelling that Phyllis had put him out. He was so angry he was spitting. He said he wasn't leaving. He said the house belonged to her and Phyllis had no right to turn him out, and he had his truck outside to take her home, where she could set Phyllis straight. They left, but she supported her daughter.

He disappeared for two weeks, then turned up with the house on Pleasant Run Parkway. A friend found it and wanted to buy it but Mike moved into it first. It was in sorry shape but a bargain, he told Trent, and what work was involved he thought he could do himself. His mother visited the house and she and his sister said they would give him money to pay for it. He had no complaints about his medication and for once he seemed to have prospects. He told Trent in the middle of August that he'd left a down-payment with the owner. He said he quit his housekeeping job and asked if he could visit Trent only once a month.

A neighbor allowed Mike to attach a hose to an outdoor faucet and run an extension cord from his basement for a couple of days, but charged him. The bearded man the neighbors saw through their windows walking the property in overalls would sometimes cross the road and disappear into the brush that grew at the edge of a creekbank and not be seen for several hours. Other times he'd drive off in his truck and return with the back of it filled with objects scavenged from trash piles. The chairs, table legs, mattresses, blender tops, and books he found he'd haul into the house, with the intention, he told people, of selling them and using the money for the renovation. His habits of living were crude. For his toilet he placed a seat on top of a five-gallon plastic bucket. He kept rabbits on the first floor. There were bales of hay in the parlor.

He asked a man who was his neighbor if he could buy his dog. The one he had, he said, needed company. He would start a conversation, then sometimes walk off in the middle of the reply. Now and then he would invite the children of his neighbors into his house and serve them cookies. He was in the habit of giving money to the children to fetch him things from the store.

He got a job in the kitchen of a hotel. A woman who

had gone to school with Mike and Carolyn and was still in touch with Carolyn worked at the hotel. She passed through the kitchen one day and saw him. Carolyn told her that if she brought Mike to a phone and dialed her number she would speak to him. He told her he was sorry for all the things he'd done that hurt other people. He said his life had not gone well, and then he described a plan to buy a farm or a house and start a commune. Carolyn said, "Did you rape that girl?"

There was a pause, and then he said, "Yes."

After her daughters heard that Carolyn knew where Mike was, they went to see him. It was the idea of the younger one, the blonde. The older went along to make sure she was safe. "All he wanted to know," she says, "was where our mother was." He mentioned the commune. He said they'd all be together and their mother could have a separate wing, "and it was weird and crazy," she says, "because he didn't have the means." Mike had spent about an hour talking to them when his boss appeared and told him to choose between continuing his conversation or returning to work, and he stayed with his daughters and got fired. It was raining and cold and he drove them back to town.

For a while he had work painting a house down the street from Skip's. Every day he would sit in Skip's kitchen over a lunch Skip made for him and direct a steady stream of complaint across the table. He hated working, he hated his job, he hated being paid so little, he hated the contractor making a profit on his labor. Then he quit.

Phyllis didn't see him for a month. He appeared one afternoon. "We had this back door that was mostly glass inside an old wood frame, and we used to leave the curtains on it open during the day, and as I walked through the entryway I was thinking, Good Lord, who is this, and he says, 'Phyllis,' and just at that moment I realized it was him, and I said, 'Mike?' His hair had got long and his beard had growed out all bushy and he was all dirty. His face was just a different color from all the dirt and his feet were filthy. He was wearing shorts and a T-shirt and flip-flops. Over his T-shirt he had on this plaid button-down dress shirt and he took that off and hung it from some metal gates we had on our porch just like some kind of flag of total defeat. When he was living with us he would take a bath every day, and you never even saw stubble on his face. I heard someone ask him later how he got so dirty and he said he was working on this house. He had this idea he was going to be like Skip and fix up houses and put people in them, and that was why he'd got it. Later when I saw the pictures of it and where he was living in this little tiny part of it— they figured out exactly what part of it he'd been living in and there was a blanket set out and some cans of food and some books and a little schoolchildren's desk—I thought it was like he was living like an animal. It was like he was a caveman. It was like he was disintegrating in front of your eyes. I didn't even open the door more than a crack and I said, 'What do you want?' and he said, 'Did your mail come yet?' and I said, 'Yeah,' and he said, 'Was my check in it?' and I said, 'No, Mike, there's no check for you.' "

THE LAYER of dirt on Mike's face, his filthy hair, the way he smelled, and the paunch he'd begun to carry alarmed Skip. Mike would appear at his door and ask for a glass of water, or to borrow some tools, or to use the phone, and would keep up a flow of requests until he managed to talk his way into the house. Skip would give him what he wanted and hope that he'd leave.

MIKE DROVE out one evening into the country to his sister Oneita's. She gave him a meal. When he left, she called his original probation officer and said the explanation for his decline was drugs. The probation officer told her that if Mike was to make it, he would have to do so by himself.

"If he's got to do it on his own," she said, "how come he's on medication? What about all the mental hospitals?"

He drove out to see his brother Jimmy and asked to borrow some tools. They got into an argument and Mike tried to strike his brother a blow with his fists. Jimmy deflected his swings and Mike got in his truck and drove off.

Modean asked Trent's advice about giving Mike money to buy the house. Trent told her something like what the probation officer told Oneita: Mike has got to work his own way out of his problems and must sometime stop relying on you to come to his rescue. He has never appreciated anything you've done in the past, and is not likely to begin to now. "Probably," Trent said, "he will simply demand more."

ON SEPTEMBER 11, 1986, Mike walked into Sacks Eagle and Loan, on Indiana Avenue, and passed a hundred and ninety-five dollars across the counter for a three-shot semi-automatic shotgun. He gave the address of the house on Pleasant Run Parkway and showed the salesman his new driver's license. When the salesman asked if he used any drugs, or had any mental health problems, or a criminal record, he said no. The salesman recalled later that Mike insisted on an automatic weapon and that he wanted to buy ammunition for hunting big animals, but the store happened to be out of it and sold him birdshot instead.

A few days later, Mike stood in his parlor, wearing a trenchcoat. Through a slit in the pocket he held the shotgun against his leg, the barrel pointing at the floor. The portion of the barrel that appeared below the hem of the coat he cut off with a hacksaw.

Modean mailed Trent a card to be given to Mike on his birthday, the twenty-third of September. "No one is *useless* in this world," she wrote, "who lightens a burden for someone else—Charles Dickens." She hoped that Mike might find a sheltered place to live, and that the money he received for his disability would pay for it. If he did, she wanted to buy him a television, for his birthday.

A few days before the murders, a Cadillac pulled up in front of Mike's house and four men wearing suits got out. Mike was not home. The men walked around the yard and went up on the porch. They knocked at the door. One of them, aware of being watched by a woman at a house next door, walked over and asked if she knew Mike Jackson. She said, "Not really. I've talked to him a few times." The man said he was a lawyer representing Mike's mother and his sister. They had planned on giving Mike twenty-five hundred dollars to buy the house, but had changed their minds. They were afraid of him and had hired the lawyer to break the news. He asked the woman if she would want to be in the position of giving him bad news, and she said, "Under no circumstances."

EVERY TIME Mike appeared at Skip's during the few days before the murders he brought a list of things he wanted.

Food or money or tools or some piece of equipment, a fuse box, say, or a piece of plumbing pipe. Skip felt that Mike had become evil. He would finesse his way into the house and stand looking askance at Skip and somehow puffing himself up so that he seemed larger than he actually was and to be barely containing a pressure within him. Skip tried not to say anything that might provoke Mike, or show any fear, because he felt Mike would sense it. When he went out the door it was as if someone had thrown open the windows of a closed and shuttered room.

Skip learned from a friend who had helped Mike saw the barrel that Mike now owned a shotgun. The friend said Mike planned to use the gun to rob people. Every time Mike came striding through the door, Skip looked at his hands.

The evening of the Friday before the murders it started to rain. One of Mike's neighbors was trying to haul a crate up onto his porch. His wife was helping him. Mike saw them from his yard and came over and said, "Need a hand?" He took the wife's end of it, saying, "You shouldn't be doing this," and he and the husband wrestled the crate a foot at a time up onto the porch. When the neighbor thanked him, Mike smiled and said, "No problem."

The day before the murders Mike came to see Skip, who was not home. Cindy was. Whenever Skip was out she locked the door against Mike. She came into the kitchen and found that one of her sons had let him in and he was just standing there. Mike had heard that Skip and Cindy collected food for the people who lived in their houses and he wanted some. She let him take what he cared to and he left.

That night around nine he went into the J. B. Market.

The way he paced up and down the aisles and stared at the register gave people who saw him the notion he intended to rob the place, or was casing it to do so on another occasion.

CAROLYN SAW Mike for the last time a few weeks before the murders. "Right before, he wrote me some nasty letters bawling me out, I mean up one side and down the other," she says. "I just wanted to see him. I missed him. I loved him and I always thought I would have given anything in the world to sit down and talk to him and ask him what had happened, and if there's a hereafter I hope I have that chance.

"I was taking a risk, and I knew it, but I don't think he would have known me if he looked at me. I knew him right away, though. From his walk. He always had kind of a cocky walk and he still had it, even run-down as he was.

"I knew he'd been in Springfield, and I knew he had lived at Harbor Lights, and I knew he was down, and I just wanted to look at him. I knew from his brother he had to go every morning for a mouth check to the hospital, to make sure he was taking his medicine. I knew he would be there at eight. I took a bus down to the hospital. I waited outside the place an hour, and then he just came out—walked down three steps, turned right, and walked away. I was about twenty feet from him. He never looked in my direction. His hair was all long and not combed and his beard was grown out, and he was wearing a short-sleeved shirt that was torn, and a pair of blue jeans that didn't fit him, and a pair of tennis sneakers. It was the first time I'd seen him with a gut; he'd always been so slender. And people couldn't believe that this was the same guy that used to polish his fingernails with a toothbrush and take oatmeal baths for his skin. Even then, though, I was wanting to go back to him. I remember standing there and thinking: he's going to meet his end in a very bad way."

A COUNTRY OF

BARKING DOGS

THERE WAS blood on the steering wheel of the Cadillac. Chief Burgess and his deputy had fired their revolvers at Jackson as he passed, heading in the other direction. Altogether they got off six rounds—Burgess four and the deputy two, before he fell back overcome by the shock of his wound. Chief Burgess, who had never before shot at another human being, later accounted for his having trouble striking a target at such close range by saying he'd had a sudden case of "shaky hands." Before Jackson's taillights were on the far side of a rise about a hundred yards away, though, Burgess registered the sight of Jackson leaning to his left, as if he had been hit.

A highway patrolman found the Cadillac in the grass between the lanes of the interstate with the driver's door open. As he approached, he heard banging on the trunk and shouting for help. Somewhere between O'Fallon and Wright

City, Jackson had pulled the car to the side of the road and made the owner get into the trunk.

THE FIRST PERSON in a position of higher authority to arrive in Wright City was a captain in the Missouri State Highway Patrol, whose name was John Ford. On Monday evening he ordered that roadblocks be set up three deep on all roads leading to Interstate Highway 70.

Other members of the Highway Patrol and agents from the St. Louis office of the F.B.I. arrived throughout the night. A manhunt is not part of the experience of most F.B.I. agents. "You'll have a case like this maybe only once in a career," one of them said later. Few younger agents were familiar at all with the idea of searching for an armed killer down corn rows and in grain bins and bean fields and didn't really know what to expect. They arrived in Wright City in their suits and went out into the rain and sank to the tops of their city shoes in muck and began pulling aside barn doors and knocking at the entrances of farmhouses.

A woman told troopers at a roadblock that Jackson had passed so close to the front of her car in crossing the highway that she nearly ran him down. In the middle of the night a man called from the trailer park half a mile west of where Jackson left the Cadillac and said that he and his wife heard the door of their pickup truck close and someone brush up against their trailer. Another man said he heard someone cough outside the bedroom window of his. The Highway Patrol sent a helicopter, which shined a spotlight on a field by the trailer park where searchers waded through grass to their waists. Others pointed flashlights under the foundations of trailers and into the cabs of cars parked beside them and, like the men in the field, found nothing.

HAL HELTERHOFF, the special agent in charge of the St. Louis office of the F.B.I. at the time, was jogging when his beeper went off. He had spent his day involved in other business, and when he called his office and was told that Mike Jackson had turned up in Wright City, he said, "Who's Mike Jackson?" Helterhoff arrived in Wright City around nine. He was reluctant to press the search that night, knowing Jackson would have the drop on anyone approaching him in the darkness. Instead, Helterhoff hoped to hear from someone who'd caught sight of a figure in his headlights, or had risen in the middle of the night and seen a shadow on his lawn, or from a farmer at daybreak viewing a figure in a field where he'd never seen anyone before. From the way Jackson behaved during the day, Helterhoff and Ford tried to predict how he might spend the night.

"You're trying to think like him," John Ford says. "Of course he's crazy, so you're at a disadvantage, but we looked at that car and saw the door open and figured he'd run, and tried to put it together. He hadn't done nothing on foot, he just stole cars. He give up one and walked away from it, and he took the next one that came along. So we just didn't think he'd walk out of there."

Manhunts are usually short-lived. A person being chased by an organization with the resources and experience of the Missouri State Highway Patrol or the F.B.I. almost always turns up in a few hours. "If we don't catch him then," Hal Helterhoff says, "we usually pull back and wait until we get a call." Helterhoff realized it would be as important to

protect the people of Wright City from Jackson as it would
be to catch him. The F.B.I. didn't want the morning to
arrive with word he had a hostage, or had killed someone
for his car—in other words that he'd continued to behave
as he had all the day before.

THE TRACKS of a freight line run through the center of
Wright City and alongside the highway at a distance of
about a quarter of a mile. The trains mainly pass back and
forth between St. Louis and Kansas City. Two trains rode
them that night. Helterhoff and Ford worried that Jackson
might have climbed aboard one as it slowed to travel through
town.

The F.B.I. arranged for the trains to run fast through the
countryside. Through town they would travel so slowly that
the lines of agents carrying shotguns and standing on either
side of the tracks would have no difficulty seeing into any
cars that were open or anyone standing on the couplings.

At dawn they swept the fields. Agents crossed pastures
south of the interstate and troopers walked in a line through
ones to the north, putting up flocks of birds, and neither
group found any trace of Jackson. "When we didn't find
him with those two sweeps," Helterhoff says, "I started to
think, We're going to be in this for a while."

HELTERHOFF AND FORD took over as a command post
the premises of the police department upstairs in city hall.
After the sweeps they were thrown back on working out
an explanation of how Jackson had disappeared so completely. They considered the trains, but Helterhoff learned
that the trains that had passed through town the night before

travelled so fast that it was unlikely Jackson got aboard one. In addition, Helterhoff figured that if Jackson had managed to escape on one of the trains, he would have jumped off somewhere, and somebody would have seen him and thought he looked strange and called the police. "He would have surfaced," he says. "He was the type of guy to be stopped by the police." Another speculation was that he had got out of Wright City by some other means; perhaps someone had helped him. Helterhoff knew from people the bureau had talked to in Indianapolis that Jackson didn't have many friends, so Helterhoff thought it improbable he had summoned anyone to help him, and Jackson didn't seem to him the kind of person who might engage a stranger's sympathy, especially in the state he was in. He's in disarray, Helterhoff thought, he probably doesn't know where he is, he's preoccupied with looking over his shoulder, and although he might steal a car or kidnap someone at gunpoint, no one says that has happened. Ford believed there was a strong possibility that Jackson had been wounded as he fled Wright City and might have crawled into the woods and lain down and died. The searchers might never find him and there would be no way to be sure of when it was safe to call off the pursuit.

BY SEVEN TUESDAY MORNING, two women had phoned the command post to say that they had seen Mike Jackson the night before in St. Charles, thirty miles east of Wright City. One woman said he had been in the Jack-in-the-Box restaurant. People in Oklahoma, and in the cities of Wichita, Independence, and Kansas City, Kansas, said they had seen him. The woman who worked as cashier in the gas station in Wright City near where the deputy was shot said Jackson had been there earlier that day. She remembered he was friendly. When she asked about the paint on his beard, he said he had been working hard lately. Then he put seventy-five cents on the counter for a package of Twinkies and left.

The first person to report a plausible sighting was a woman who called the command post early that morning to say that she and a friend had been driving along the interstate the night before and through the darkness and rain saw a man running across an overpass west of town. The overpass is perhaps half a mile west of where the Cadillac came to rest. The man was headed north. Helterhoff and Ford decided to concentrate the search on the woods and farms and fields and houses north of the highway.

CITIZENS:

"Monday evening we got stopped at the roadblocks, we were hit in the face with these bright lights. Come to find out they were the lights from a television camera, and our friends called and said they saw us getting our trunk searched in Wright City. Well, I don't know anything about that—we didn't see it—but the agents would come up and tell you to open your trunk, and they'd stand *way* back with their guns, and you'd go to open it and wonder, Now, wait a minute, why am *I* standing up here opening the trunk, if they're way back there with the shotguns?"

"I know it was a Monday, because I equate it with 'Monday Night Football.' It didn't really seem like a big deal at first. I had friends on the fire department—you know they hear things over the radio first—and this one guy called up and told us the situation, and there didn't seem that much to it, and then 'armed and dangerous' come down and *that* made people sit up a little."

Wright City had a high school and an elementary school. They drew students from the surrounding county and between them served nine hundred children. On the first day of the manhunt about three hundred children stayed home. Some people, such as a waitress in a restaurant called The 50's Café, took their children to work. Before the school buses left in the morning an F.B.I. agent walked the aisles, pointing the barrel of a shotgun between the seats. Agents with shotguns boarded the buses twice along their routes, then the buses were searched as they passed through the roadblocks. Before school opened in the morning agents with shotguns went through the buildings, opening doors and turning on lights in dark rooms and peering into closets. Once classes began, all doors but one were locked. Anyone passing through the unlocked door did so under the eye of a guard with a shotgun. Having children caught in a cross fire or one taken hostage was what worried everyone most. What accounted for there being slightly less concern for security at the high school was that everyone felt it didn't pay Jackson to grab a child the size of an adolescent. The kindergarten class cancelled a trip to a berry farm. The school was locked at three. All sports and activities scheduled to take place after school were called off. No one wanted to risk the children's being out after dark, or even at dusk.

Tuesday the delivery of mail was suspended. The carriers whose routes lay through the most isolated parts of town didn't want to go out, fearing that Jackson might jump from behind a tree or a barn or anywhere so long as their backs were turned, and take them prisoner or kill them for their car.

Bea Kee is postmistress of Wright City. "We had one female carrier that didn't want to go out Tuesday morning," she says, "and she was crying and one of the other women carriers had just got a gun and she said, 'How about I go with you?' and I said no. I thought all I needed was a car with one girl at the wheel in tears, and another in the back seat pointing a shotgun out the window. Later in the week I let one of the husbands go with a couple of them, which you're not supposed to do, but I had permission from St. Louis."

Ms. Kee expects complaints when the mail is late, but no one said a thing.

John Ford told reporters covering the search that the longer it went on the greater was the likelihood that Jackson had left Wright City. He said, "He's wet, tired, and hungry. He can't stay in hiding forever."

All day Tuesday F.B.I. agents and state troopers crept toward farmhouses, barns, outbuildings, silos, and any pile of brush that appeared large enough for a man to hide under. They performed barrel rolls and ran zigzagging lines across open fields, as if they were soldiers under threat of fire. They wore clothes with camouflage patterns and carried twelve-gauge shotguns, which they called thundersticks. Throughout the day they struggled to stay calm as fox and raccoon and deer bolted from hiding all around them.

People began to say that Jackson had driven toward Wright City with the barrel of his shotgun in his prisoner's mouth and his finger on the trigger.

ABOUT THE FIRST THING a lot of people did was take down a gun from its rack or the top shelf of the closet or the drawer of their bedside table and carry it with them. It was not uncommon for people without handguns to carry rifles in the front seat of their cars. One man spent Tuesday on the steps of his trailer with a twenty-two rifle. Another leaned against a car in his driveway, embracing a shotgun. An experience that unnerved the drivers of the school buses was the sight the first morning of children at the bus stop waiting among fathers holding rifles and shotguns and pistols.

"People were all buying guns that never had them before, and everyone was really on edge," says Bea Kee, the postmistress. "I had one woman to tell me she was going to shoot anything that moved after dark and I thought, Oh, boy."

Tuesday night people turned on all the lights in their houses and on their porches and in their driveways and yards. Some replaced the bulbs from their outdoor lights with more powerful ones. They sat in their houses with guns in their laps. Men walked their grounds and their downstairs rooms with rifles while their families slept.

TWELVE HUNDRED PEOPLE live in Wright City. Chief Burgess patrols a territory two miles long and one mile wide. In the center of town is a crossroads. The buildings around it are mainly flat-roofed and without details and as many are empty and out of business as are occupied. No one building rises much above any other and none stands taller than three stories. Church bells in town play hymns. Men drive by in pickup trucks with raised suspensions, their heads about level with that of a man in a saddle. The roads run straight to the points of the compass, rising and falling with the roll of the hills so that a car coming toward you in the distance appears and then disappears, like a small boat rising and falling in the trough of a wave. The light that falls on the fields at the end of the day, after the farmers have left them, is rich and dramatic. The edges of the sky extend so far that you can see weather on the horizon before it arrives. Storms bend the trees. Hawks riding the currents of heated air above the fields sometimes rise so abruptly that it looks as if they were being lifted by strings.

In their beds people imagined Mike Jackson walking the tree lines between fields and down the swaying aisles of corn.

THE SEARCHERS continued to wonder whether he was gone. Agents rode some of the trains but no one saw him. Ford and Helterhoff felt that to board a train Jackson would have to get close enough to the tracks that someone on the train would catch sight of him, but no one who worked for the railroad said that he had. Two of the bullets Burgess and his deputy fired at Jackson went through the door of the Cadillac, and only one was recovered. "They didn't know," says Burgess, "if he hadn't crawled up some brush pile and died, 'cause of that bullet, which they never found it in the car."

The F.B.I. took pictures of the landscape from a plane and used these to divide the fields and woods into grids they could search systematically. Some of the grids were as large as a square mile of open terrain and some were specific to the yards and barns of a farm. A highway patrolman described the activity of walking up to barns and farm sheds and grain bins as being like "going around with your heart in your mouth."

Chief Burgess: "Any old shift of the wind, or breaking

of a branch, or creak in the floor, just an ordinary sound you wouldn't pay no attention to it before, now it was something. It grew up into Mike Jackson and people was calling me all the time with some kind of bulletin, they seen him somewhere. Everything that was normal became exaggerated."

On Wednesday mail was delivered to all but the most remote parts of the routes, where there were few customers anyway.

THE DAUGHTERS of Earl Finn, the man Jackson shot in his car on the highway, asked that an autopsy be performed on their father. No explanation his family could come up with seemed to account for what had happened to him. Even if he had suffered a heart attack, he wouldn't have left the road so abruptly. The doctor performing the autopsy discovered the birdshot. Inside Finn's car were found then the wadding from the shell and holes in the roof from stray pellets. Not until a search of the car Mike was driving turned up a shotgun shell were the authorities certain they knew what happened.

When Helterhoff and Ford learned the extent of Mike's rampage they summoned additional agents and troopers. By Wednesday there were sixty troopers and sixty federal agents in Wright City, or one searcher for every ten residents of the town. Technically the F.B.I. wanted Jackson for shooting Tom Gahl, a federal officer, while the Highway Patrol wanted him for shooting the policeman in Wright City.

MERCHANTS in Wright City who had citizen band radios could hear the truckers on the highway warning each other to stay clear of the town. Travellers without the benefit of the truckers' advice could see the roadblocks. The owners of restaurants presided over empty dining rooms. Pumps at the gas stations sat idle. The merchants burned. The barber in Wright City has a sideline selling guns. People would stop to talk about the manhunt, or perhaps ask about a gun, and end up getting a haircut.

A television station in St. Louis broadcast Wednesday that Jackson had checked into a mental health clinic in Dallas, then they retracted the story. Someone in town said that Jackson's remains were discovered in woods on the outskirts of a farm, and someone else said Jackson was hiding with relatives in a part of Wright City called Beeny Hill.

At six that evening, agents and troopers searched a house in Laddonia, forty miles northwest of Wright City, in which there was living a man who once shared a cell with Mike Jackson.

FOR SOME PEOPLE the chance to walk around with a gun and the possibility of using it on a murderer in self-defense was a kind of answer to prayer, but many others were uneasy over the idea of loading a revolver or a shotgun or a rifle and preparing to point it at someone and pull the trigger. It wasn't that the thought of sitting helpless in their houses after nightfall made the accommodation any simpler, but it was enough to convince most of them that arming themselves was sensible and necessary. "We're not gun kind of people," says one man, "my family, I mean. I had a twenty-two rifle from my grandfather and I remember getting it down Wednesday and putting a shell in the chamber and thinking, this is crazy."

People in the country began to lock up their houses and

leave. Some moved in with relatives in town, some to motels, and some left Wright City altogether. Occasionally a searcher would arrive at a house and find a note on the door, saying, "We're gone, call us at sister's," or "Moved to in-laws." Wednesday afternoon a young couple were reported missing. Their car was not in their driveway and neither of them had shown up at work. For a time it seemed to Helterhoff and Ford that they had heard from Jackson, but the couple were eventually found at the house of the young man's parents in a different county.

Speculation arose over whether Jackson in his flight had any destination in mind. Perhaps he was headed to Springfield for revenge. Or to his homeplace in Mississippi. Helterhoff tended to think Jackson had no plans other than to lose himself somewhere. A highway patrolman said what Jackson was doing was anything he needed to in order to survive and when anyone presented himself as a threat Jackson killed him. His neighbors in Indianapolis worried that he might return. "This guy is a survivor," one of them told a reporter. "He's lived his whole life as a loner, taking care of himself. We saw him living that way here. If he wants to come back here, he'll make it."

Toward evening Ford and Helterhoff would address the pool of newspaper and television reporters who spent the day outside the command post waiting for information. On Wednesday Ford told them searchers had spent much of the day knocking on the doors of houses around where Jackson was last seen. He said everyone was tired but spirits were high. Searchers were still combing the low ground and brush near the highway and by the railroad tracks, on the theory that Jackson had been wounded in the exchange of fire. "There's no sign he has left the area," Ford said. "His mode of operation is to move, take hostages, and kill people. He's done none of that that we know of since Monday. If he's out in these woods somewhere, I'd say he's hurting."

F.B.I. offices around the country were told to watch for Jackson, in case he had slipped through the manhunt. While the F.B.I. had no reason to be sure he had left, they also had no idea where he would go if he had.

ANYONE IN WRIGHT CITY who took the appearance of Jackson casually, or felt inconvenienced by the searchers and roadblocks, began to be stirred toward different feelings when the first descriptions of his exploits and character arrived. What they heard through their televisions and radios and read in their papers was that Mike Jackson began a crime spree in the ninth grade that took him most of the way through the rest of his life, that he abused alcohol and suffered an addiction to heroin, that he was believed to be schizophrenic, was carrying a shotgun, and that before walking into a small grocery store (very much like the one in Wright City) and killing the owner for failing to do what he told him to quickly enough, he had sprayed his face with silver paint.

"If he's found a home where someone might be on vacation," John Ford said, "he might be living in fairly comfortable style. If he's been out in the woods, he's got to be pretty uncomfortable. If he gets desperate for a drink of water or something to eat, he may tip his hand."

Mike's sister, Oneita, said she felt Mike had been headed toward a catastrophe, and that she and the rest of her family had more or less been waiting for it to occur. She called him "a living dead person," and said that he was filled with hate and wanted the rest of the world to suffer as he had. The deputy who had been shot said he hoped that one of his bullets had struck Jackson, and that now he was dead and couldn't hurt anyone else anymore.

A woman reported seeing a man through the rain near the rest stop on the interstate. She said he was wearing a maroon shirt, but when the searchers arrived where the woman had said he was standing, they found a wet cardboard box. By Wednesday fifteen people said they had seen Mike Jackson in St. Louis. The command post also received many reports of guns being fired, and of people seen running across open fields.

Chief Burgess sat down that afternoon to make a record of all that had gone on so far in the search. He hadn't slept much since Jackson arrived in Wright City and fired his shotgun at the car he was sitting in. "Excitement kept you going," he says. What he found was that so much had gone on and so little was familiar that he was able to recall almost none of it.

ON WEDNESDAY Helterhoff called for dogs to be brought to Wright City. The first to arrive was a cadaver dog, whose talent was for locating corpses. The dog was taken to where the Cadillac crashed and let run for a day through the fields and woods. He found the carcasses of a rabbit, a goat, and a cow. The handler told Helterhoff he considered it very unlikely that the body of Mike Jackson lay anywhere near at hand.

Karen Girondo, who works at city hall: "As soon as the F.B.I. and the Highway Patrol arrived and the command post set up, I got my parking space at city hall taken away and my phones taken too. We weren't supposed to answer them, and they'd ring upstairs and someone would answer and say they never heard of you and hang up. It totally disrupted the functioning of the city. We just couldn't function as a city at all." (John Ford: "We took *over* the town. The people in the city hall there couldn't even make out a water bill.") "The woman who worked for me couldn't come in after a few days from the pressure. She got a doctor's note not to come to work.

"There were some people that didn't pay it any attention at all. They let their kids stay home alone. But they were in the real minority."

Among that minority were some of the families who lived on farms south and west a few miles of the town. Mike Jackson had arrived in Wright City during the harvest. When a person expresses surprise at the idea that people living in the most isolated parts of town, in houses from which you can't see any others, might decide to put up with the thought of a murderer crossing their fields and hiding in their barns, he usually hears the response "You can't walk off a farm."

Some farmers carried guns. Some sat on their tractors, raising their eyes to the edges of their fields. Some believed that having never harmed Mike Jackson, no harm would come to them. One farmer shelling corn expressed this thought to an F.B.I. agent. The agent said, "He shot a man never knew him just was driving home from work."

One woman tried to keep Mike Jackson from her home by praying. Meanwhile her husband walked the rooms of their house with a butcher knife.

A taxpayer: "Mayor Roland Springmeier had a thirty-aught-six in the trunk of his Cadillac. Now how was he going to get to that thing? He'd have to pull the switch on that trunk and walk round to get it. I said, 'Why you doing that?' And he said, 'Well, you got to be prepared.' And I said, 'Mayor, that's the sorriest thing I ever saw you do. What's going to happen if you see him? You going to put him on hold, while you get your gun? You want to be prepared, you keep that thing up there cocked with you.'"

BY WEDNESDAY police were looking for Jackson to appear in Pontotoc. The F.B.I. figured he had nine shells for his shotgun, the clothes he was wearing, and the rings he stole from the woman he'd held captive with her son. Whatever else he needed, they assumed he could find.

Ford and Helterhoff went on thinking that even if Jackson survived being wounded in the gun battle, his wound would be liable to infection.

Chief Burgess said Wednesday that the search for Mike Jackson had turned Wright City into the safest town in America. Someone happened to ask where his family was, and he said that he sent them out of town to stay with relatives. "I can't be home to protect them," he said.

By Wednesday the searchers were weary of the barrel rolls and the zigzag runs. It became an effort to remind themselves that Jackson might be around the next corner, or over the next rise. A trooper told a reporter that the search could continue without any end. "I'm not being hunted," the trooper said. "He is. I'm the hunter, and he's the huntee."

Helterhoff and Ford were concerned that Jackson might

shave and change clothes and pass through a roadblock. "He has at least one advantage over us," a trooper said. "He's going to know us before we know him."

The F.B.I. agents began to discover that their money was no good in Wright City, which made them uncomfortable. Members of the congregation of the First Baptist Church started Wednesday night to carry coffee and food to agents at the roadblocks. Much of what the parishioners delivered came from donations made by restaurants and stores in Wright City and in Warrenton, the next town west. Later in the week the church took over the responsibility for feeding the searchers. The parishioners set up a kitchen in the command post and fed the agents and troopers as they returned from the field.

Sightings, Bill Hollenbach: "The first night we saw him, there was this limb down in my backyard and we were watching some movies. We saw this shadow on the grass —we had the outdoor light on—and after a while it moved 'cause he stood up, and we watched him walk across the backyard over to the fence and across it and down the fence line to the woods."

Chief Burgess: "When I would see a likely place I would just check it out; I didn't really have a schedule or route or tell anyone where I was. I was mainly doing spot searches. 'Cause it was pouring down rain and you couldn't really get out and look around much. I concentrated on about a two-square-mile area where he was last seen, give it the local angle. You always ran into the other searchers, you always knew they were there. A lot of people thought they had a good idea about where he would be, but none of them was right.

"Meanwhile people would call in suspicious sightings. They'd want you to come check out their yard, and you didn't come in time, they'd escalate it, make the story a little bigger, to try to get you there faster. Lots of people were reporting suspicious individuals—hitchhikers, someone stopped in from the highway, anybody they hadn't seen before. I even had two or three people to report a black man. One man said he saw Jackson three times. I believe he probably saw him once and invented the other two."

THE F.B.I. began using a plane, called the *Nightstalker*, which carries equipment able to detect the warmth of a body. The equipment was developed by the military during the war in Vietnam. The plane took off each night from St. Louis and flew above the fields and woods of Wright City. It was painted black and flew without lights, so that in the darkness people could hear it above them, but not see it. The F.B.I. preferred to keep the existence of the plane confidential. The people in Wright City knew it was there and what it was doing, but the F.B.I. would not admit that such a plane existed.

Bill Hollenbach, again: "The next night we were watching movies and we heard this tapping on the wall. Then I heard him at the door, and I actually believe I saw the door handle turn, and that's when I got a shot off."

Cookie Stude, a citizen: "Right from the first night I slept with my automatic rifle next to my bed—I have an automatic that'll go seven rounds. I didn't have the clip in it, but I kept it by my bed.

"Every evening and again in the morning my husband would move the hay bales around in the barn to see if anyone had been in there messing with them. Feeding the animals first thing in the morning and throwing open those doors when you didn't know what was behind them, or who might be in the corners, was tough. Before you got in your car you checked the backseat and you knew as you sat there that the car was locked, still, you always expected someone to come up and grab your shoulder. It was just pure fear. And driving you found yourself really gripping the wheel. You would drive down a road you had travelled comfortably hundreds and thousands of times before, only now you would feel you had these iron-piercing eyes on you. You didn't know when you were imagining it and when it might really be true. He surely had eyes on some of us."

THE AGENTS began to think he might have spent time in trees and weren't sure they hadn't walked under him. They tried not to think of how tired they felt and to believe in the confident, he's-here-somewhere attitude of their leader, but some of them, as they stood in a downpour soaked to the bone, found it the simplest thing to conjure an image of Mike on a bed in a motel room somewhere out West, steam on the bathroom mirror from the hot shower he had just taken, wrappers from a hamburger joint on the carpet, and him watching a movie on cable TV.

"We started to think he might have got a car," says Chief Burgess. "There's a lot of farms out that way with old pickup trucks or farm trucks in the barns, and you got weekend places out here people only come to occasionally, and we thought maybe he'd got to something like that, taken a back road and somehow got clear of the roadblocks. Or he could just have walked out of there. It's not hard to see the roadblocks and he could have stayed away from them. He could have seen any cars coming at night—you can't drive your car without the headlights—he would just have to jump out of the way. But there wasn't any indication from anywhere that he was operating. The F.B.I. had the place covered, I mean here was a guy who was used to holding up liquor stores for cash and we didn't have any reports of that. I believe they had a report of a boat stolen in Louisiana, and that didn't really fit the case, but that just shows you how well the F.B.I. had this thing covered, that they knew about a boat missing in Louisiana."

While there was comfort in knowing Jackson hadn't appeared to have turned up anywhere else, it was troubling to acknowledge that the only time Mike Jackson had been heard from at all was when he was taking a hostage, stealing a car, killing someone, or trying to.

FIRST ELDERLY WOMAN: "They came in one night and searched my whole place, upstairs and down. They even searched my kitchen cabinets. Now, how's a man going to get into my kitchen cabinets?"

Second elderly woman: "I opened the door one time, there was a knock, and I could see out the window all these F.B.I. men in the parking lot pointing guns back at the apartment building, and I peeked through my glass and saw a federal man on my doorstep and when I opened the door he was pointing a gun at me and there was two more on either side of the door and *they* were pointing guns at me. I tell you I went white down to my feet."

A waitress at the truck stop: "My son worked at the Pepsi plant, that's just west on the South service road, and he has a beard and he's about twenty-one at the time, and he was heading out to work and he had a '66 pickup truck and it was needing all kinds of work and it was down to the primer in places and he was doing all kinds of things to the body, and he stopped at the roadblock and they asked him for some identification, because of the beard, and they didn't know who he was, and he had a soda can between his legs and he reached down to move it, and he didn't even almost touch it when he said they had three shotguns right under his chin, and one of them agents was saying, 'Don't you move, sucker,' and he told me, 'Mom, I didn't even twitch.'

"He was going to come check on me once, he said I want to see how my mom's doing—he was living in Wentzville—and I said, 'You stay where you are, they're liable to shoot you with that beard.'"

A customer at the truck stop: "They pulled my son one time right out of his truck, due to his beard. He was going up the service road. He's only seventeen but it was dark. Them wearing camouflage clothes."

A citizen: "My brother lived out there about a mile as the crow flies from where Jackson crashed that car, and him and his wife moved into town with my parents. I mean this is a forty-two-year-old guy, a Vietnam vet, and he gave up and just moved into town. And I remember we went out to his house to pick up fresh clothes and you know you open that door and stick the gun barrel in first. I remember thinking, This is crazy, we're going to shoot each other.

"We're a commuting town, you know, get on the interstate and drive into St. Louis, and he was a liquor salesman in downtown St. Louis, and his wife—they're divorced now, they didn't have any kids—she worked at the bank and she'd be home out there and he'd have to be worried about her alone in the house and they just gave up.

"I mean it really just disrupted the routine around here. She was used to coming home at lunch, watching a couple of soap operas, and going back, and you couldn't do that. Not only did you not want to be home alone, you didn't know who was in your house when you got there. You heard all *kinds* of sounds at night and it didn't take no trick of the imagination to build one of them up into more than it might be. All it took was one you'd never heard before. One guy got so nervous, he shot out his patio window. *Boom!* He was sitting there watching TV, with his rifle on his lap, and a shadow moved, or his dog barked, or he heard some sound that spooked him, and he shot out his patio window.

"After a while the rumor mill started going. And I mean they made this guy out like he was in*visi*ble, like you couldn't see him, or know where he was, or think as good as he could. And then the folk hero thing started, you know, that maybe someone was helping him. People around that time were starting to get real, real down on the F.B.I. because this thing was going on, and they started to think the idea that some guy could get away from all these people in such a small area seemed like it should be impossible, a fantasy. They were saying, 'Bring down the National Guard, and do this thing right.' People when it started were bringing the F.B.I. cookies and fresh, baked cakes and Kool-Aid, you know, because it was hot, and the church was taking them meals, but that kind of enthusiasm all began to taper off. People were saying, 'They're using this as a training exercise. They know exactly where he is, but they're bringing these young guys out and letting them get a taste of this work,' and, you know, after you heard that and looked at those guys they all *did* look kind of young.

"And it got very eerie when it turned dark. I can tell you that. You didn't know *where* he was. The F.B.I. agents were everywhere, standing there at the roadblocks with these jackets on saying 'F.B.I.,' and they checked you everywhere. After a while it got familiar and sometimes they would just wave you on, but it sure slowed things down and it was upsetting seeing men with shotguns standing around all the time and the helicopters coming and going all night, all the time, making all the noise. I heard some of the guys who had been over in 'Nam saying they were starting to get pretty upset with those choppers landing and taking off all night, with the sound that they made, and going along in the darkness with their lights sweeping across the fields and the tops of people's houses like some kind of search-and-destroy thing, and I have to say I don't blame them."

Men and women would walk up to the searchers and say, "I hope you find him, and I hope you kill him."

A TELEVISION STATION in Mississippi found Modean. She appeared seated on a couch and she spoke in flat, measured tones. "Mike should not have been loose," she said. "I tried to get him confined at two or three different places and they didn't keep him. For years he hasn't been able to cope with society and he should have been kept confined."

The F.B.I. published a poster saying they wanted Mike Jackson for killing a federal officer. The poster included a picture of Mike taken in jail in 1985 when his beard was full and his hair was long. The contrast between the white of his face and the black of the beard is so intense that the image looks like an inkblot on a Rorschach test. Beside it was a photograph from 1986 which had been manipulated to suggest what he might look like with shorter hair and beard.

The New York Times described Wright City on Thursday as existing in a "virtual state of siege." A woman told a reporter she found little comfort in the idea that Jackson might be dead. "We're scared," she said. "But it's the fact that no one sees or hears anything out there that's really scary. Is he hiding out there? Is he dead? Or is he gone?"

Chief Burgess said he found it a "weird feeling" to be shot at. He described Wright City's crime rate as being "about as close to zero as you can get." Only two murders had taken place in his memory. One by a hitchhiker who stopped off from the highway, and the other by a man in a fight with his daughter's boyfriend.

In the evenings people in town would call friends and relations in the country to see if they were all right. When they got no answer, they would get in their cars and go look for them. Returning to their houses after shopping or running errands or from work, people would stop at the command post and arrange to be accompanied by an F.B.I. agent, who would search the house before they went in.

Werner Strick, the minister at the First Baptist Church, said that along with fear and anger people felt compassion. "We also pray for the mother of that lost and hunted son," he said.

BY THURSDAY most of the students who stayed out of school had returned. The schools were still locked and guarded. No recesses or gym classes were held outdoors.

The open house at the elementary school and the chili supper at the high school were cancelled. The superintendent said that children held out of school during the manhunt would be allowed to make up the work they missed without penalty.

Each day, agents and troopers dressed like soldiers came and went from the command post. Helterhoff and Ford stood on the pavement in front of city hall and told the reporters, We have no reason to believe he has left the area, we think he's lying wounded somewhere, if he's out there he's got to be awfully uncomfortable, and sooner or later he will do something to reveal himself. The details of the hunt—whether the searchers believed they were close, or as much in the dark as they ever had been—they kept to themselves.

Not long after midnight on Thursday a man stopped his pickup truck at a roadblock and told the agents he'd just had a fight with a hitchhiker he had taken aboard on the interstate. The driver was a marine, twenty-one years old, on leave from boot camp. He was bleeding from his nose. He said he had managed to kick the hitchhiker out of his truck and that the man fled into woods up by Warrenton, the next town west. The hitchhiker, he said, had a beard. To have as many men as possible involved in the search, Helterhoff and Ford called everyone off the roadblocks.

A waitress at the truck stop: "We live up in Warrenton back there—do you know Warrenton? You know the Wal-Mart there? Well, behind of that there's a subdivision, and our house is on the last road there and back of it is some woods. This marine told the F.B.I. that Mike Jackson stopped his truck on the road and tried to take it from him, then ran, and they thought he'd got into this woods. It was about two-thirty in the morning and we have these sliding glass doors in our bedroom that look out on woods and we heard this tapping on the window and this man said, 'Ma'am, are you all right in there?' and I didn't say anything—he said he was from the F.B.I. but we didn't know—and he said again, 'Ma'am, are you all right in there,' and my husband spoke up, and the F.B.I. man said, 'Okay,' and we went to the window and looked out and we could see about six guys, wearing those green clothes that they wear in the army, you know, and some had 'F.B.I.' written across the backs of their jackets and more of them were walking up and down the street and they had the helicopters up there and they were shining lights from it down on our house and across the lawn and the bushes and the street and over our neighbors' houses and the woods. And we have this little dog and from the yard down to the end of the street he don't want nothing going on unless he knows about it, and Pooh-bear, he started up yapping."

Her husband: "They was tapping on the window and wanting to know if she was all right, and I said, 'Yeah, we're okay,' and they said, 'Ma'am, are *you* all right?'

"I sat up the rest of the night, walking the house with my shotgun. I told my wife and kids, 'You hear any shots, you hit the floor,' because anybody try to come through that door I was letting them have it. That was a scary time. The F.B.I. was right up on the porch tapping on the window before we ever heard them, or the dog either, and if *they* could do it, well . . ."

The agents and troopers searched for three hours in the backyards and garages of the subdivision and in the woods in back of it and found no trace of Mike Jackson. They brought dogs to the place where the marine told them the hitchhiker fled. The dogs ran back and forth but not forward. The agents turned to the marine, who admitted then he had got into a fight in a bar and to avoid trouble with his father invented the hitchhiker.

Some agents felt that the experience of pulling people from their houses in the middle of the night and scaring children to tears with the sight of armed men dressed like Ninjas running across their backyards in the darkness and shadows while a helicopter with a searchlight hovered above them—all of it for no reason—added up to the lowest point so far of the search.

What preyed on the minds of Helterhoff and Ford was that Jackson might have used the occasion of the roadblocks being down to escape.

During the search the F.B.I. found two people who said they saw Jackson open the Cadillac's door and run for the woods. What else the witnesses told them that they hadn't known for sure was that no car stopped to help him.

IT BECAME inevitable that the searchers would pull the handle on the door of the same outbuilding and poke their flashlights into the attic of the same abandoned farmhouse more than once. The alternative was to press the search farther in all directions. Doing so, they might run past him or spread themselves so thin that they had no effect. If Mike Jackson was in Wright City, they meant to draw the circle around him as tight as they could. In the minds of Helterhoff and Ford the most convincing sighting was the one given by the women who said they saw a man in the darkness heading north across the overpass. The fields, woods, farms, and the town itself, which lay to the south, were searched, but not as intently. Pictures taken from planes of land to the north showed a number of abandoned cars, in which Jackson might find shelter, and also a junkyard, which was as tedious as a maze or a warren to search. Covering the same ground made the effort to keep everyone alert more demanding. In addition it was hard to tell if a footprint, or a door left ajar, was evidence of Jackson or a searcher.

"Your search area gets contaminated," says Chief Burgess. "After a while they don't know who's been through it. Me and my deputies sometimes would be out riding, and we'd see a barn and think, that looks like a good place to hide, and we'd go search it, didn't tell no one we was there, so you don't know how many people have been through a place."

Most people stayed out of the woods, except squirrel hunters. "They weren't looking for him," says Chief Burgess, "yet some people you can't break their habits, they're not going to be intimidated off their routine."

BY FRIDAY the people in town were accustomed to the armed men and the roadblocks, but still were unnerved by the sight of each other carrying guns. "It's a miracle more people didn't get hurt around here," says one man. "You didn't go knocking on *anyone's* door at night, unless you called first. Kids had guns, women on their own had guns, girls staying by themselves after school while their parents were at work had guns, *every*body was buying guns, and I am just petrified of guns."

Everything the F.B.I. did it kept secret, at least partly

from a fear that some piece of information might give a citizen the idea he could pick up his gun and go and find Jackson himself.

"There was talk of people getting together and hunting him down," recalls one man, "two or three hunters banding up and going out to find him, because people were getting real frustrated with it, real testy. I mean to say, it was your freedom being taken."

Friday morning the F.B.I. and the Highway Patrol handed out the poster with Mike Jackson's picture. The owner of the Wright Stop, a grocery in town, taped one to his door. He said that he wanted life to get back to normal. "People are restless," he said. "It bothers you every night when the sun goes down." No one went anywhere at night if he could help it, and no one cared for working alone. A man who owns a car lot says, "I had a guy working for me, and sometimes I'd have to leave on some piece of business and he just locked up when I was out; he wouldn't even open the door. Wouldn't go out on the lot to check the cars if it was dark. I don't even know if he answered the phone."

The searchers planned to use a bloodhound on Friday but couldn't locate a track for the dog to follow, so gave it up. Fifty policemen searched a freight train a hundred cars long in Griffith, Indiana, because someone told them Jackson might be aboard, but he was no more visible there than he was anywhere else. A woman drove around Wright City with a sign in her window that said, "Michael Jackson with your silver crown, we don't want you in our town."

Searchers scanned the sky for vultures, but whenever they went to see what the birds found they located only dead animals. A number of people had come to feel sure Mike

Jackson had left. At the command post and the roadblocks and out in the fields the searchers would ask each other, "Do you think he's here? Or he's gone?"

A policeman stuck a dowel through a bullet hole in the door of the Cadillac. The dowel passed through the armrest and came to a stop against the rib cage of a trooper in the driver's seat.

"We figure there was no way he couldn't have gotten hurt," announced Ford. "He was sitting in the driver's seat and got hit. There's no doubt in my mind." He described Jackson's probable wound as "a gut shot."

On Friday Helterhoff and Ford decided they had worn out the land north of the highway. Whoever it was the women saw on the overpass, it did not seem likely it was Mike Jackson. Perhaps they had confused the time and the man they actually saw was someone already searching for Jackson. Given the thoroughness of the searchers, it did not seem possible they had overlooked him, so Helterhoff and Ford decided to turn the search toward the land lying south of the interstate.

At night, the agents and troopers at the roadblocks would sit in their cars with the lights off and not turn them on unless someone approached. During the first days of the search they asked every driver for his license and to open the trunk of his car, but over time they became familiar with the people whose routes to town or work they were obstructing and the exchanges became less formal. People learned that the men on the roadblocks really hated it when you approached with your bright lights on. They also learned that the best way to get cheerfully through was to turn on your interior light. Some of the roadblocks were easy to pass, but occasionally a television cameraman would arrive and then the agents would turn people out of their cars and put on a show, and the people knew the difference and resented it.

NONE OF THE DOGS that went out on Saturday turned up a trail. A man and his wife in Calwood, forty miles west of Wright City, came home to their farmhouse to find that someone had eaten two pork steaks from their refrigerator, and some peanut butter from a jar. The intruder had taken supplies from a first-aid kit and slept in their bed. He also bound three rifles together but left them behind. Fingerprints on the rifles sank the F.B.I.'s hopes.

Shooting into bundles of newspapers, agents tried to determine what damage Mike Jackson suffered from the bullet that penetrated the Cadillac's door. "We're confident he's still in the area, but he could be dead," said a spokesman for the Highway Patrol. "We're sure he was wounded."

Someone in Wright City saw Mike in a field and shot at him. When he didn't move, the person went closer and discovered he had fired at a tree stump. Agents in Mississippi, Texas, Louisiana, Arkansas, and Oklahoma checked reports that Mike had been seen in their states. He was reported looking through a window of a farmhouse near Valparaiso, Indiana. Agents flew in a helicopter over the woods and fields around the farmhouse and also above the landscape by railroad tracks nearby, where someone said they had seen him jumping from a freight train.

On Saturday afternoon a young man showed up at a roadblock by the interstate and asked how to get to the command post. Once there he asked where Mike Jackson might be, and the agents searched his car and found two rifles and a shotgun in the trunk. The young man turned out to be Mike Jackson's nephew, his sister Oneita's son. He had come from near Indianapolis. He told the F.B.I. that his uncle was an outdoorsman and could survive on his own for days at a time. He said Jackson was "a naturalist" and an avid camper and hunter. He also said his uncle had a suit of body armor, and the F.B.I. wondered if that might have protected him from the bullet they knew to have struck him. The F.B.I. assumed the nephew came to help Jackson escape and they took away his guns, but then they let him go.

"He went down there to put a bullet in Mike's head," his mother told an acquaintance a few years later. "He was a sharpshooter. We tried to talk him out of it, but he said, 'Ma, he's my uncle, and I'd rather shoot him before anyone else did.' He thought Mike was like an animal that was suffering and he was going to end his pain."

AS FAR AS ANYONE KNOWS, Mike was actually seen only once, by a man named Paul Godt and his brother-in-law, who were standing in the drive of Godt's house about a mile south of town and watched him cross a field.

"This was Saturday afternoon," he says. "I was working outside with my wife and my brother-in-law, who's a conservation agent and has been involved in manhunts before, and it was about three o'clock and we were boiling apples to make apple butter. We're on a lake, and on the other side is a field, it's kind of gently rolling land, and I looked over—it's about a hundred and fifty yards—and there was this man walking briskly across the open field. He was taking big wide steps, and walking just about as fast as you can before you're running, like he *knew* he wasn't supposed to be there. He had black hair, he had his left side to us, and his left arm straight down along his side, where maybe he was carrying his shotgun by his leg so we wouldn't see it. He had his jacket tied around his waist with the arms knotted—I could see that plain as anything—and he went across the field and stepped over the fence at the far end by the creek bed and travelled down into the woods.

"My brother-in-law was the first to see him and he said, 'That looks like the guy they're hunting.' For Jackson to cross that field took about thirty seconds. That's how long we watched him. He was in a real hurry and he turned around and looked right at my brother-in-law, with his eyes on him. And I knew it wasn't anyone I knew. No one had permission to be in that field and I only have my neighbors on the other side of the lake—the farmhouse at the end of the lake is abandoned, I own it—and I called him and asked if he'd been out there, or given anyone else permission to be, and he said no.

"Where Jackson was walking was just under the ridge. You see, Highway F, which is a county blacktop, is right over that rise on the other side of the field he was crossing, and if he'd been above that ridge he'd have stood in plain sight to anyone on that road.

"I called the F.B.I. and I was a little angry at how long it took them to get here. I don't know if it didn't sound all that good a sighting to them, or if they had too many other things to look into, but it took them about forty-five minutes or an hour to get here, and when they did they only sent two agents, and they just walked across the dam of the lake and looked around.

"Sunday morning my brother-in-law and I went over and found his tracks. That field was usually in corn but that year it was soybeans, and the combine had been through a day or two before, so it was down, and my brother-in-law studied them and guessed he weighed two hundred pounds from the depth of his track compared to ours, and from what I saw later on the poster, that was about exactly right. So Sunday I went back to the office because I really thought I had a legitimate sighting, and I guess when I came back a second time they began to think I did too."

After that, a car was often parked at the end of his driveway and sometimes he would come home from work and his neighbors would tell him there had been a string of patrol cars outside his house while he was gone. Or he would find cigarette butts here and there in his yard and out by his garage, though no one in his family smoked.

AT DAWN on Sunday, agents and troopers left the command post for the countryside carrying county plat books that gave the location of every house. Their plans were to knock on the door of each and ask the people who answered if they had seen Mike Jackson and to make sure that no one had been taken hostage. Where they found no one home, they left a note asking the person who lived there to call the command post.

Buzzards circled over woods near where the Cadillac had crashed and a cadaver dog was sent but found no corpse. Dogs trained to follow cold trails, and dogs trained to follow hot ones, were presented with clothing brought from Mike's house, then taken to the fields, but no dog gave a sign it had turned up his track.

John Ford took a seat in the front pew of the First Baptist

Church of Wright City, where Preacher Werner Strick led a prayer asking that Mike Jackson be brought to see it was best to give himself up and "end all the turmoil."

The Indianapolis *Star* ran a story describing the feeling in town on Sunday under the headline "Besieged City Living in Terror of Fugitive." Anyone who wondered how to estimate the threat of Jackson's presence had only to note that none of the searchers ever entered the woods without an automatic rifle and a bulletproof vest.

People drew their blinds. A man and his wife moved into their bedroom once night fell, because the curtains in their living room were sheer. Another couple moved to their living room to be close to the door.

Real estate agents gave up showing houses in the country or any near woods. People lined bottles along the sills of windows in their basements. They shot at dogs they couldn't see that moved suddenly in the brush. They sat at night in the shadows of their kitchens, drinking coffee.

The press and the searchers often identified Jackson incorrectly as Michael, which made a number of small children think the pop singer was after them. Most parents kept their children indoors. Some wouldn't let them walk from their cars to the door of the school except with an escort. A girl who could see a shed in the backyard from her bedroom developed the idea that Mike Jackson was in the shed and hasn't been able to go near it since. Kids stayed away from the woods, for fear he could be lurking in them. One girl playing at dusk by woods in back of her house took in the movement of a shadow with the corner of her eye and ran back to the house and didn't leave for three days. Boys at school carried scissors in their pockets and pencils sharpened to points. Families rehearsed drills designed to get them out of the house in case Mike Jackson arrived. Every morning the farmers rose and stared out their windows at what they could see of their yards and the paths to their barns and tried to put out of their minds the thought that Jackson could be in their corn or sheltering from the rain in their barn.

Everyone shuddered at the thought of being taken prisoner.

SUNDAY AFTERNOON a man called the command post who owned a trailer that sat among a grain bin, a shed, and some derelict cars on a piece of property south of town about three and a half miles. He had left the trailer several days earlier without locking the door, but when he got back to it the door was locked. Two cans of soup in the trailer and a can of sausages had been opened and the contents eaten and the cans put back on a shelf. Someone had heated a pot on the stove and put it on the bed. Clothes were moved in such a way that it appeared they'd been tried on. In the minds of people who had dealt for a week with hoaxes and bad sightings and false alarms, none of this evidence stirred much excitement. The details that raised the hopes of the searchers were these: someone had shaved with disposable razors, and in the sink were dark hairs flecked with what looked like silver paint.

The agent who came to lift fingerprints found none he could read. The process by which a laboratory might determine whether a hair was Mike Jackson's required that the hair be attached to its root. "Yeah, it could be just about anybody," a spokesman told the press, "but I don't know how many burglars would come in and shave." Helterhoff and Ford now felt certain Jackson was alive and had not left Wright City. The men in the fields, whose spirits had been flagging, also felt renewed.

The only ambivalence felt was by some citizens. "There for a while they had us feeling safe thinking maybe he was dead," a farmer recalls. "That lasted about four or five days, and then he came back on us."

A discovery at the trailer that preyed on the minds of Helterhoff and Ford was that ammunition for a rifle was missing. Someone once reported Jackson to have a rifle, as well as the shotgun, and the truth couldn't be determined. If he did have a rifle, a person searching for him was in more jeopardy than if Jackson had only the shotgun. Helterhoff was afraid that any order he gave might lead to the death of one of the searchers.

The F.B.I. brought to the trailer a dog that ran through fields toward the highway and town. It left the trailer around four o'clock, heading north. The tactical team from the St. Louis office of the bureau followed, wearing camouflage clothing and heavy vests and carrying their weapons. A helicopter flew above them. The dog crossed the driveway of an abandoned farmhouse where there were sheds and falling-over barns, turned east, crossed a two-lane black-top—Highway F—entered fields, crossed a narrow wood and a pasture, came to a pond and followed its edge, then turned north and after about a quarter of a mile came to the end of a dirt road and a pond and a house by itself that appeared to be empty. The F.B.I. searched the house and two barns on the property, and then the dog turned west, running through a field alongside the dirt road that led to the county road, and when it reached the pavement it turned north and headed straight for Wright City. The day was hot. Raising their knees high to follow the dog through fields of tall grass and woods and up and down hills and through thickets of brush wore down the searchers. The largest member of the tactical team, the bodybuilder, tired and had to have his rifle carried by one of the others.

Running alongside the highway through front yards and past houses and cattle barns, the dog entered town, turned east, ran beside the railroad tracks for a few hundred yards, crossed them, then ran down an alley toward the command post. Agents at the command post followed the search over their radios and as the dog came closer to Wright City proper they said, Damn if that thing don't come right past us, and as they leaned out the windows on the second floor watching, son-of-a-bitch, it did. Where it stopped, around six o'clock, was at the back door of an empty Victorian house down the street. The house belonged to the local mortician who intended to restore it for new premises.

As night fell the F.B.I. began searching buildings in the center of town. People who earlier in the day left their houses in the subdivision on the far side of the tracks were kept from going home. As they stood at the roadblock looking across the tracks at their houses about all they could hear was a police radio now and then or one of the searchers pumping a shotgun. The roadblock was lifted at nine-thirty and people went home. A boy who waited with his parents at the train tracks refused to sleep alone that night in his room. "He might be outside my window," he told his mother.

While agents and troopers were shaking the doorknobs

of buildings in town and shining their flashlights through the windows, Helterhoff and Ford were considering how to search the house. Someone was sent to find Doug Brown, the mortician who owned it. "They came over to my house," he recalls, "and told me I was wanted at the police station, and I thought, Well, what have I done now? Most of my work takes place at two or three in the morning, people just seem to die more often at night, that's just the way it is in this business. I do the embalming for several places in the county, so I was used to the roadblocks from seeing them then, but I couldn't imagine what they wanted to talk to me for. When I got to the command post it was around nine o'clock and they didn't really tell me what it was for, but they were wanting to know about the inside of this old house. So I sat down with them and thought hard about it, and the harder I thought the less I realized I knew. They wanted me to tell them about the floor plan, and I said, 'That's easy, it's over there in the basement,' and they said, 'Well, you're not going over to get it.' So I went through it a floor at a time with them, as clear as I could remember, and I realized later I had overlooked a lot. There was a kind of big flower box area on the first floor by a window, big enough for someone to hide in, and I forgot totally about that. They were mainly wanting to know which way the doors opened, and of course, I couldn't really remember that—I never paid it that much attention—and where were the closets and places where a person could hide. One team would come to me and say, 'We're going in the back door, what's there?' And when I finished with them, another team would come and say, 'We're going in the front, tell us about that.'

"I stayed with them from nine till about through the next morning. Once I got in there, they wouldn't let me leave, I don't know why. I worked with the SWAT teams from about nine to midnight and the rest of the time they were getting the people evacuated who lived in the houses around it. They didn't want anyone around if there was gunfire. There were about twelve or so families and single people to take care of. The sheriff or somebody would call, and mainly they were old women, and it got to be about three in the morning, so you can imagine how they felt when the phone rang and it was somebody on it they didn't know, and he would tell them something like, Three men are coming, they'll have guns and don't say anything, be as quiet as you can and go with them. I owned the houses on both sides, so I knew who was living there, and one tenant just wouldn't answer her phone, then I finally remembered she was away in Webb City for the weekend, so that held things up."

By four in the morning, thirteen families had been evacuated from twelve houses around the empty one. The assault was planned for just before dawn. Rather than go back to their hotel rooms, the members of the St. Louis tactical team lay on the grass outside the command post to sleep.

The television people hoped to record the assault but Ford and Helterhoff had them and the newspaper press escorted across the bridge above the highway and kept there, where they couldn't see anything but the roof of the house. The agents going into the building were dressed in black. If the television crews turned their lights on the house, the figures of the agents would show up like targets in a shooting gallery to Jackson inside.

"The head of the team from St. Louis was giving instructions about who would go where," says Joy Strick, who was serving food, "and what window you'd take, and when the dog would go in, and it really surprised me, they were nervous—I guess they don't do this all the time—and I remember there was one guy who was so fidgety he just couldn't even stand still in his shoes. And I was watching this and thinking, I never in my *life* thought I would see anything like this, and then as they were about to go I suddenly realized this was not television; they were going out and they could get shot, and they might not all come back."

The eight agents from the two tactical teams, one from St. Louis and one from Kansas City, left the command post single file according to the order of the task each was expected to perform. Kansas City was to clear the basement and St. Louis the first floor and so on through the three floors to the roof. They carried stun grenades, which make a noise so loud that it gives the searchers a second or two before the person they are seeking returns to his senses. The dog they brought was trained to search rooms for anyone hidden. He belonged to a policeman from St. Louis. When the policeman was asked if he understood his dog might be killed, he said that if the dog helped to save someone's life he could survive its death.

A member of one of the tactical teams: "The owner of the building said, 'Break down the door.' It had this beautiful big oak door and we didn't want to ruin it, so he found a key and we snuck up on the place and stuck the key in, and of course it didn't work, so we had to break down the door anyway."

Doug Brown: "When they got in they went pretty fast, one group up the front stairs and one up the back, and you could hear them on the radios saying, 'First floor's secured, we're going up to the second.' They'd send the dog ahead and follow. Where they thought he might be is up in the attic, because from there you can see the police station. Also, I think, there's a window up there and it was loose at the time and there were some drapes in it and they would move with the breeze and it was spooky and I think that kind of fueled their imagination. All the doors were locked and the windows shut, but there was a coal chute in the basement and from outside it looked like a window except it had no glass and they would shine their lights on it and it wouldn't reflect back and they thought that's how he had got in there.

"I think they were real disappointed when they got back. You could see they weren't really looking forward to *shooting* the man, but you could tell they wanted to find him."

The tactical team member: "There were all these old women living around the house there, and they were all giving us hugs as we left, and weeping, and the women making food at the command post too, and I felt kind of sheepish going back after that big send-off. I guess they got to that house with the dog and he started sitting down, or sitting up, or turned around, whatever it is that they do, I guess he was pretty excited, but if Mike Jackson had been there, he'd left some time before."

The rest of the day people in town were saying to each other, "Wright City, wrong house."

HELTERHOFF AND FORD, uncertain what to do next, decided to take down the roadblocks, in the hope Mike

Jackson would notice and make a move that someone would see. They sent patrols consisting of an agent and a trooper to rove the countryside and visit people who had something to report. About two dozen searchers took part in these patrols at any one time. Others worked in the command post, answering phones, planning strategies. The other hundred or so mostly went back to their motel rooms and lay down.

A spokesman for the Highway Patrol said that the search had been reduced because "we didn't have any new leads and we've already looked everywhere we knew to look." Another trooper said that after the search of the house in Wright City, "We're right back where we were a week ago." Some of the troopers were given time off. The Highway Patrol was concerned that if the search kept going much longer with the troopers working seven days a week and having to be given compensatory time there might not be enough of them left to patrol the state through the end of the year.

Later that morning the tenant who lived above the funeral home came out his door and found one of the dog handlers and his dog checking the garage across a small parking lot from the house the agents had searched where the mortician parked his hearse. The handler said, "He definitely stood on the back porch here."

DURING THE FIRST WEEK of the manhunt, in Mississippi and Tennessee and Missouri and Indiana just about anyone who was related to Mike Jackson, or had grown up with him, or hung around Indianapolis with him, had lent him money or lived nearby him, shared a prison cell with him, treated him as a patient, or overseen him as a prisoner was visited by a member of the F.B.I. In addition, agents gathered hospital records, prison files, letters, drawings, and any other material they could get their hands on that they thought might be revealing of his personality and sent it to an office of the bureau in Quantico, Virginia. Agents there used it to predict how Jackson might act. By the second Monday Helterhoff and Ford had a number of these predictions in hand.

The agents thought Mike would spend the bulk of his time either sitting or lying down. The rest he would devote to searching for places to hide. Where he would feel most comfortable would be under bushes, or concealed in spaces just large enough to accommodate him. Spaces two and a half feet high and three feet deep they thought he might find the most appealing.

He would not steal money, since he had no way to use it. He would probably have very little to do with anyone; more likely he would take pains to avoid people, unless, perhaps, he found an elderly black couple just managing to get by. People such as that he might not think of as threatening and might trust for food and to protect him.

After three to five days the place where he was shot would be infected and painful and draining of his strength. The discomfort would only be worse for living outdoors in the rain and mud, and the strain on his faculties would reduce him to a level of survival as anxious as an animal's.

He was most likely to move in the hour before dawn and just after dark. He would cross a small road, but not probably walk along it, which meant that he was likely to be seen only briefly, if at all. He was apt to walk in circles, and to race from one hiding place to another, like a rabbit in a brush pile, or, like a deer, to run twelve or fifteen steps in one direction, then stop and take stock, perhaps while crouching on his haunches.

Whatever rest he was taking was likely in the form of a catnap. He would probably avoid empty houses, thinking they were places the police would expect him to be, but he might nap in the outbuildings of a farm. Having learned that he often slept in his car, they felt he would be comfortable resting in cars he found abandoned in the countryside, especially any near ravines. He might also sleep on straw.

The need for medicine might draw him toward town. He might break into a doctor's office and steal bandages and drugs or possibly hit a drugstore. Except for medicine or food, or perhaps for shelter, he would probably stay clear of town. On the occasions when he stole, he would take little enough that whatever it was would not immediately be recognized as missing. If no one reported anything stolen or his house broken into, it probably meant Jackson was foraging. Hog pens and cow barns and grain bins were places he might look for food. The fields of course were full of soybeans and corn. Even so, without skills to find nourishment and survive outdoors, a week without shelter would be punishing.

Planting false information about the search in the papers, or presenting people on television pleading with him to give himself up was not likely to work, since he was probably not reading the papers or watching television.

He was apt to be very frightened. He might perhaps be as much a danger to himself as to someone else. Being flushed by searchers, or perhaps a farmer coming across him in his barn or by his fields, is how he would most likely be found, and if that happened he would probably not hesitate to shoot. Given the chance, he would probably steal cars, take prisoners, rob stores, and kill people. He was not likely to cross prominent barriers, such as the highway, or a streambed, partly for fear of being seen and partly because he might think of them as boundaries marking territory he might feel it unsafe to enter.

He would not call a friend and ask to be picked up. He would always have his gun with him. If he were chased from a field to a house he would take captive anyone in the house. He would not negotiate. The end would be violent. He would probably not be taken alive. There would more likely be a gunfight. As someone whose mind was given to constructing conspiracies, he was likely to feel particular distress, even anguish, at the idea that the world was pursuing him.

Having made themselves familiar with the predictions, Helterhoff and Ford turned to the map of Wright City on the wall of the command post and both saw the same thing: the territory into which they now believed Mike had run —that is, the terrain south of the interstate, the landscape that included the trailer—was enclosed by roads. The area within them, however, was not insignificant, several square miles, nearly all woods and land without houses. Also the railroad ran through it, and the agents at Quantico had sent no predictions about trains.

ON MONDAY Oneita spoke to a reporter for a paper in St. Louis. She said Mike was a "stickler when it comes to cleanliness." She said, "Mike all his life had to have his hair just so and his teeth and body clean." She described him as "cunning," and said that he probably knew how to take care of himself in the woods. He had spent his life overcoming the obstacles of one situation or another, and it would not surprise her if he was able to once again. She and her family believed that Mike might be toying with the searchers. "He can backtrack." she said. "He's got them all baffled. They need an Indian scout. You just don't know where he is going to end."

EARLY THAT AFTERNOON two agents from the St. Louis office went with a dog handler to see if the dog could find any trace of Mike Jackson along the bed of the railroad tracks. They started west of Wright City, in a place about halfway to where the Cadillac had come to rest. The dog ran toward town. It followed the bed of the railroad for nearly a mile and when it came to a field at the edge of the town proper it stopped before a derelict shack with a front porch by itself on a rise. The dog sat down thirty yards from the house and wouldn't go closer. The handler said that was very unusual. The house stood as isolated in the field as a small island in the center of a lake. The agents crept up to it and kicked back the door and jumped through the windows, then went back to their hotel rooms and lay down.

Some of the searchers began to wonder if the dog that led them from the trailer into town might not have been running backwards.

ON MONDAY a man driving a truck to Kansas City from Indianapolis stopped in Wright City and drew a crowd when he said he was Mike's brother Jimmy. He was short and wearing a plaid shirt and western-cut dark pants with a silver-plated belt buckle the size of a paperweight. He had gray hair that was parted on one side like a schoolboy's and held in place by a tonic; only a wind strong enough to raise his collar disturbed it. His face was small and shaped almost like a heart. He mostly kept his hands in his pockets. His voice was deep and he spoke quietly and when he cleared his throat he excused himself. His eyes found the spaces between the shoulders of the people he was talking to. He told reporters that he was sure Mike was alive somewhere, but not in Wright City. He could have shaved and found new clothes and look like a "completely different person than he was when he came here." He said that Mike always had a violent nature. "He's my brother," he said, "but he would shoot me in the back just like he'd shoot anyone else." He was pretty sure that the police would have no luck finding Mike, that even though Mike had no training in how to survive outdoors, as far as Jimmy was aware, he was operating on the instincts of an animal and those would be sufficient to see him through. Jimmy felt that Mike was "pretty slick," and said that for the last twenty years all he had been studying was how to get away from the police. Of their fight, he said, "I just blocked his blows. If I had known what he was going to do I would have knocked him silly."

Jimmy spent an hour at the command post, answering questions and delivering the opinion that the drawing made by an artist at the bureau to show Mike as he might look with his beard shaved off was not a good likeness. They asked him to listen to a recording of a call a paramedic in Warren County heard around three o'clock that morning on the band of the radio the police use for mutual-aid calls.

The caller said, "I've got your man, I've got one of your cars, and I'm leaving the state." Jimmy did not recognize the voice.

JUST AFTER NIGHTFALL Monday several agents concealed themselves in the fields around the trailer. The agents had glasses with lenses that allowed them to see in darkness. Each agent carried a small light which emitted a beam that could be seen only by someone wearing the glasses. This would allow them to distinguish themselves from Mike Jackson, should he show up again.

That night the command post received the second report from a man in Seattle that Mike Jackson was hiding in a barn in Marthasville, Missouri, ten or twelve miles south of Wright City, on the Missouri River. Tactical teams from St. Louis, Kansas City, St. Charles County, and the Highway Patrol stormed the barn, and that was pretty much it for the seventh day of the search.

BY TUESDAY the anxiety of the manhunt had sufficiently unsettled people in the town that they were holding meetings where they discussed how they were feeling. Mainly frustrated and weary and hopeless and angry. The man who owned the market said that the manhunt was making people jumpy and irritable, and that the effects were much worse than when it began because it had gone on for so long. A woman dreamed he was under her trailer. "He's out there somewhere," she said, "he's just watching us."

Tuesday evening, the *Nightstalker*, on its way to the route it had selected to patrol, picked up an indication of a man in a field about three quarters of a mile north of the trailer.

In the center of the field was a creek bed down which an agent crawled, pulling aside brush and choking on the dirt and dried leaves stirred up by the blades of a helicopter above him. Agents walked beside him down either side of the creek, but none of them found anything. The *Nightstalker* operates by orienting its equipment to the bearings of the landscape it is searching. The evidence of the figure in the field arrived before it had done so. Once the equipment was oriented properly it identified a different field; the agents concluded that they had been sent to a field about half a mile west of the one in which the figure was detected.

A farmer: "They were looking at the creek branch one night with all the helicopters flying over with their lights, and they came to me and asked did I know of any caves along that branch or overhangs, and I said, 'Well, not that I'm aware of,' because this is all soil in this country, we don't really have any rocks, but they were having a problem I guess with that plane, they were able to spot him sometimes on their screen and I guess he would just disappear, and they thought maybe he was ducking into some caves. But some of those draws are pretty brushy and maybe he was just curling up under some of all that. I told them that they should put agents out like they were deer hunting, in tree stands, and just wait for him to come by."

WEDNESDAY the governor arrived to assure the people that the state would not give up the search. He said that he would call out the National Guard if Helterhoff wanted, but Helterhoff said he thought the F.B.I. would be able to find him. People reported seeing Jackson in St. Clair, Missouri, and at the Pony Express restaurant in Miami, Oklahoma, and agents went there with photographs. Two men from St. Louis drove out to Wright City and reported seeing Jackson in a field. Searching the field, a trooper climbed a tree and fell out and broke his wrist and the men were arrested for filing a false report. A reporter visited an Asian woman who owned the motel in town and she showed him her register. "Look at this," she said. "Last month, all these people; sometimes full. Not now. They come in and ask about police helicopters, and we tell them, 'Murderer,' and they leave. Only F.B.I. and some people from New York stay."

That afternoon the Department of Justice added Mike to the list of "Ten Most Wanted Fugitives."

"Born September 23, 1945, in Pontotoc, Mississippi," said a press release, "Jackson is described as a 5-foot-11-inch, 210-pound white male with brown eyes and brown hair. Jackson reportedly has scars on the crown of his head and across the knuckles of his right hand. . . ."

The reason for Mike's being placed on the list was the fear of his having shaved and picked up new clothes and left Wright City altogether.

A TRACKER

IF MIKE'S SISTER had known that there actually was
such a person, she might not have suggested so publicly that
what the F.B.I. needed was an Indian scout. In sending out
a call for more dogs, Helterhoff heard from the tactical team
at the bureau's office in Knoxville, Tennessee, that they
occasionally trained with a man named JR Buchanan, who
lived in the foothills of the Great Smoky Mountains and
was adept at following tracks. Helterhoff told them to bring
him, and he arrived on Tuesday.

Buchanan had been taught to track by his uncle and
grandfather, who had trapped in the Smokies. When a coon
or a fox broke the trap line and dragged off its trap, someone
had to study the ground for signs of which way it had gone
and get back the trap. An animal like a raccoon or a fox is
light enough that it leaves little sign of its passing. Perhaps
it will turn over a dry leaf, which will be darker on the side
that had been facing the ground, or bend a blade of grass,

or leave behind a broken twig or some bark where the trap got stuck on a branch and the animal chewed the branch to get free. Once he became accomplished at detecting this kind of information, Buchanan felt that tracking a person who had stolen a trapline was easier.

Buchanan's full given name is JR. He is in his sixties and retired as a ranger from the park service. The bulk of his career he spent in the Smokies tracking ginseng diggers and lost hikers and poachers of deer and bear and wild hogs. Poachers were the most numerous and posed the most complicated problems. A poacher will brush out his tracks with branches; he'll backtrack; he'll walk on rocks and logs or through streambeds, and when he leaves the stream he'll turn around and walk out backward, or walk up to one and back in. Or he'll deer-walk—that is, lift his feet straight up and down so as not to scuff any leaves or pebbles or pull down any ferns or undergrowth, whose broken stems might reveal his trail. If a track is a day old, there'll be no sign left of a deer walker. Also, because they have guns, poachers are more dangerous. Buchanan sneaked up behind them and grabbed them. Sometimes they dropped their guns and ran and then all he had to do was get the name off the gun or the fingerprints and make a phone call. One time he crept so close to a poacher who was waiting for a deer to come through a gap that he peered over his shoulder and read the time off his watch.

Buchanan is small and reserved. To gesture emphatically he will sometimes narrow his eyes. His voice is pitched low and is raspy and flat and his speech is unhurried. He has a Southern accent but the hill twang in it is local to eastern Tennessee. When he talks about what he might do with his

life after he is too old to track he says, "When I retar . . ."
He has the habit of inverting certain words. He says, "Ever
who did it," or, "Ever which one of you has to look for the
trail," or, "Put your skill up against ever what you're hunting." When he comes to rest he nearly always lights a cigarette and chomps down on it as if it were a cigar. Wherever
he has stood any length of time there is often a small ring
of cigarette ends. His hair is long on top but thin enough
that you can see through the strands of it to whatever is
behind him. He usually wears a cap. His patience has limits.
He once grew so exasperated with a man who was relying
on a map and a compass in country Buchanan knew by
heart that he held his gun beneath the map to draw the
needle of the compass to the direction he wanted it to point.
He lives in a part of the Smokies called Happy Valley in a
house he built for himself. He used pine for the frame and
poplar for the siding. The poplar has been turning blue. He
says this is because it was cut at the wrong time—poplar
cut on the light of the moon won't turn. Because he has
spent a lot of time travelling and living in other parts of the
park on assignment he has occasionally returned home to
find his house broken into. After he lost a new refrigerator
he decided to do something to protect his possessions. He
was a demolition expert in the army and he rigged the doors
and windows of his house with explosives. By the door he
uses to enter the house is a small, hand-lettered sign that
says, "Warning. This house is booby trap with C4. Befor
you enter please have a long talk with God. ?." Beneath the
notice is a drawing of a skull.

In his time in the woods Buchanan learned a lot about
animal behavior. A bear can twist the top off a mayonnaise

jar. An old wise bear can make holes with its nails in the side of a soda can without spilling much of the soda. Wild boar nearly always arrive first at plane wrecks in the Smokies. They show up almost immediately and root in the dirt near the wreck. Buchanan spent so much of his career protecting deer and bear that he can no longer hunt them. About the only animal he has no feeling for is a tracking dog. He says their noses get stuffed up and stop working after twenty or thirty yards on a dusty road, and they work poorly after a rain.

Buchanan came to the attention of the Knoxville office through an agent there he trained. Other agents, particularly ones on the tactical team, thought knowing how to track could help them catch fugitives. Buchanan liked the agents and enjoyed laying out trails for them and setting up ambushes along the way. Of the agents in the woods he says, "That was one of the dumbest crowds you ever see. They didn't know but two kinds of trees: ones standing up and ones laying down. But put them in the city . . ." Buchanan and the tactical team devised a formation for tracking so that he could trail criminals while the agents covered him. The first time they would be putting it to use would be in Wright City.

"It was on my off days," Buchanan says. "I was down here in Happy Valley whenever the F.B.I. started calling and my wife and daughter was at home, of course she told them where she thought I was at, they called the ranger station, they called everybody that they could think of, to see if there was anyone who had seen me, and there was one house they didn't think of, and I was there talking to the man and his wife, and I started home and got into

Gatlinburg, and the Gatlinburg police blinked his blue lights and pulled up beside me and he said, 'You are wanted at home *now*.' He said he'd clear the road for me as far as the city limits. So he called the deputy that was just a short distance from the city limits and told him that I was a-coming through and I got on home. Of course my wife come out, my daughter come out, and Larry Barnett, my boss, and his wife. Time I got stopped they were standing there waiting. All four of them started talking at the same time. I said, 'Now just one of you talk and tell me what this is all about.' Larry said, 'The F.B.I. is a-waiting on you,' my wife said, 'Your bags is packed.' I said, 'Well, I'm tired and sweaty and I got to take a shower,' and Larry said, 'Make it fast.' He was my boss. I said, 'Well, I'd just like to know what is going on.' He said, 'There's a killer on the loose in Wright City, Missouri, and there's a plane on the runway waiting to take you.' So I grabbed my bags and throwed them in the patrol car, and we headed out to the airport, of course running under blue lights the bigger part of the time. We got there, the plane was sitting there a-waiting on me, been there about four or five hours. Bob Swabe, he was one of the F.B.I. agents and he was to be my partner tracking, I had trained Bob about five years, and he explained that the man loved to kill people—I believe he had already killed three and wounded a policeman there in Wright City with a shotgun, that's what he liked to use—and he told me that the SWAT team from Knoxville was already waiting for me, and he had trained all them about five years.

"Anyhow we got there way in the night and a-raining, which it rained all the time I was there, that country's like something else, that mud turns to glue, you get that in your clothes or on your boots you don't ever get it off, it *stays*. The most of the people that lived out in that country had moved into town, they had just dropped everything. I believe it was the second day I picked up the tracks. They took us out on a side road, right close to where he had been seen last. They'd been out there hunting him with dogs and some grid searches, but he didn't stir during the day. I tracked him for, I guess, about a mile. They said they hadn't been nobody in that area, so I was pretty sure it was his tracks, which it was after we got him. He went into a barn lot and walked on through the lot into the driveway of the house. And in the driveway was a car with a note. What I remember of it, the note said, "A full tank of gas, a thermos of coffee, and some sandwiches, please take them and leave." He had walked up to the car but he didn't touch nothing, probably maybe afraid it was poisoned, I don't know. And he went on about two hundred yards to a blacktop and that's where I lost him. You just can't track on a blacktop, least I can't. That was getting down late in the evening then, so we started out there on a stakeout that night for the planes to work. They had pulled in a special plane that was equipped with I don't know what, but anything that had heat, it picked it up. It picked up I *know* a rabbit, and flying over a pasture it picked up of course the heat from the cattle, and the cow piles they had just dropped, he picked that up. But they never picked up no human, except the ones that was on the stake-out, he picked us up. So we went back in and got us a little rest at the motel, and next day we started out again.

"It was a little west of where we'd lost the tracks. We went up and down the road, but, with that hard rain, and he could have stayed on the blacktop a couple of miles, which I think he did, he didn't leave no sign. So we had checked some old houses and a whole lot of outbuildings and a lot of rolls of hay—they had a lot of that stacked up, we were a checking that—and long late down in the evening we come to a big farmhouse, and we called in where we was at and what we were doing. I had the whole SWAT team around me, and I'm going forward with one of them in front of me, one on either side, and one in back, like a diamond, this was the pattern we'd worked out, because I can't look up to see where I'm going, or what's in front of me, I got to keep my eyes on the ground, and just then my partner called me over to where he was at, and he said, 'I found a track.' This was about a quarter mile from where I'd lost him. Of course it was a-pouring rain, but he knew where to check for tracks. Some of them will stay, they'll look old, but in that mud it stays, it might fill up with a whole lot of water but your track is still there. He showed it to me and I said, 'That's a tennis shoe, probably a half hour old, to judge from the rain in it,' but he said, 'I can't find any more tracks.' I said, 'Well, you stay behind me, I'll see if I can find any more tracks.' Meanwhile we had them call on the radio to the agents that had checked that house earlier in the day, to see if any of them had been wearing a tennis shoe, and none of them had. The track was right there, once in a while maybe the grass had come down and hadn't come back up, maybe a blade was broken. It was heading up toward a big barn, the barn had some farm equipment in it, so I tracked him I guess, between two and three hundred yards. It took about ten minutes, I was moving pretty fast. He had went to the soybean field, between the house and the barn, where he had collected I believe five or six of the soybean stalks and a plastic bottle of dingy pond water; there was a little pond there. So from there I went going on to the barn and in the drive of the barn, just inside it, there was a plank laying there with a wet track on it. I told the SWAT team, 'He's here, we've got him.' It was getting, I guess, about an hour before dark. I said we would need some strong lights, we're going to go up after him. They had checked the house already and they had been checking the barns too on the days before, but they had not checked the barn yet that day. We got the lights, one of the F.B.I. agents had them in the trunk of his car. And we went on and I told the SWAT team, 'Anything that moves, I want it dead, I don't care if it's a rat or a mouse,' and I spoke big and loud, so the man could hear me. I had three agents right with me. The man had one way in and one way out, the whole barn was closed with galvanized roofing. Why I said that was because I was the one in front and I was the one who was going to get killed first, I knew that; he would probably shoot me first. So we started up into the loft.

"We didn't get into the loft.

"The tracks are right up on the rungs of the ladder where he had climbed into the loft—I'm putting my hands on them as I'm climbing—and at that time there was a shotgun blast went up. I didn't know if he had shot one of my partners, or if he had raised up on them and they had shot him, or if he had shot at me and missed. So we all hit the ground, me and the three agents, but they got out. I was farther toward the back of the barn, and I got tangled up in some farm machinery there, I believe it was a scratcher of some kind, and I dove into a stall, still not knowing what that shot was all about. Finally Bob, my partner, and I.V., one of the agents—they called him I.V., that's what he goes by, always has, it's his initials I guess—they had got to where I could talk to them and they said none of them was hurt, wanted to know if I was. I heared one racket while I was hiding there, and that was right above me, it sounded like you scoot your foot forward in the hay. Anyway, they said, 'We've got to get you out of there.' I said, 'There's only one way out,' and I.V. said, 'We will give you cover, when I count to three, we're going to open up, you come out,' and when they opened up with shotguns, I came out."

The property that included the barn was on a piece of higher ground about a mile south and west of the town. A white, two-story, tin-roofed house stood broadside to the road, toward the front of the land. The curving border of a field of soybeans edged the yard. Behind the house were a collection of sheds and swaybacked barns, the largest of which, and the farthest from the house, was the one JR Buchanan had fled. The Highway Patrol determined the first shot to have been fired at 6:23 Thursday evening.

While Buchanan was approaching the barn, agents were searching the house. Within the catalogue of sightings reported that day was one of a man in a blue raincoat. Two agents searched the house earlier in the day and recalled seeing a blue raincoat in a bedroom upstairs. When they went back a few hours later, it was gone. One of them walked toward the barn, which had a lean-to shed at one end, and as he got closer to the door the hairs stood up on the back of his neck. He turned around and went back to the command post with his partner to let the tactical team know about the raincoat. They arrived at the house with a dog about the same time as Buchanan and the team from Knoxville.

Once Buchanan and the Knoxville agents were clear of the barn, they set up a circle in the fields around it. The reason for keeping their distance was the recollection that ammunition for a high-powered rifle was missing from the trailer. The vests they wore to protect themselves would do no good against fire from a rifle.

It occurred to them that they couldn't be certain who was in the barn. It might have been someone out with a gun for whatever reason who heard them coming and thought they were Mike Jackson. As unlikely as it seemed for anyone else to be shooting at them, they didn't want to look like fools for announcing they had him and then finding they were wrong, or worse, victims of a hoax. As they stood in the fields in the fading light trying to figure out how to approach the barn, they heard a sound like someone stamping his foot and some pigeons came flying out.

Meanwhile, the Highway Patrol and the F.B.I. blocked the road that led to the barn. The reporters were kept by the railroad tracks about a quarter mile away. As night fell they could hear a man's voice amplified by a bullhorn coming to them over the fields. "I know you're hungry," it said. "Talk to me, Mike; we don't want to hurt you; I know you're tired, we all are." A spokesman told them that agents had surrounded the barn and tried to negotiate a surrender. "Voice contact was made," he said, "but the subject wouldn't come out. We don't know for sure that the subject is Jackson." John Ford told those who remained at the command post, "We don't know what condition he's in. He was still able to communicate with us thirty minutes to an hour after six twenty-three."

A number of the agents who had spent eleven days looking for Jackson were tired and wanted to rush the barn and get the thing over with, but their superiors persuaded them to calm down. A fear the searchers entertained was that Jackson would somehow be able to escape in the darkness. They couldn't close ranks tightly enough to be sure that he couldn't, because that would mean coming close enough to the barn that they might be within range of a rifle. Once night fell two helicopters moved into place above the barn. One kept a searchlight on the barn as steady as possible, but the wind kept tossing the copter, so the effect of the illumination on the barn at times was almost like that of a strobe light.

When it became clear that Jackson couldn't be talked from the barn, a plan was drawn up to send tear gas into it. In the loft at the barn's south end was a window. The F.B.I. figured they could shoot tear gas through the window and not have it come out the other side and gas the searchers there. A marksman in the field fired a test shot at the window which struck the side of the barn a few inches from it. He adjusted his aim, then sent seven canisters of gas into the barn. When nothing happened the F.B.I. began to wonder whether Jackson hadn't managed to protect himself behind a barricade of hay. Another explanation was that tear gas sometimes fails to produce its effect on mental patients. Or perhaps Jackson had turned up a gas mask. No one wanted to go into the barn and get shot full of holes. Of course Mike Jackson could also already be dead. As they reviewed their recollections of the shot, some agents thought they heard pellets striking metal, and the only metal they knew of was the galvanized roofing.

The F.B.I. planned to wait for daylight to enter the barn. Although they believed that they had the advantage in a night assault, they also felt that they had spent eleven days finding Mike Jackson and it didn't seem to make any sense to race through his capture and risk a mistake. The reason they decided to rush the barn in the darkness was that a storm was approaching. A rising wind made it difficult to keep the helicopters in place, and the lightning and heavy hail they expected made it dangerous to leave the agents standing in an open field.

The agents considered lowering grappling hooks from the helicopters to the roof of the barn to pull it off. The man who was renting the property told the F.B.I. that if they wanted to burn down the barn it was all right with him. Instead, they got him to make a drawing of the interior. Then they gave it one more try with a dog. They had a dog that was trained to attack, which is what it kept trying to do to almost everyone it met, but when they sent it into the barn it came out after five seconds, which was considered an ambiguous response. Around eleven o'clock the tactical teams assaulting the barn—one from the Highway Patrol and one from the St. Louis office of the bureau—lined up in the bean field, on the southeast corner of the barn, where there were no windows. As with the house in town, each man stood in the order of the task he was given. The Highway Patrol team was to clear the floor. The first man in the F.B.I. team had a grappling hook to pull down the hay bales. Two men followed with long poles at the end of which were mirrors, so that they could stand on the floor of the barn and see into the loft, where Mike was, if he hadn't moved. The two men who came after had the responsibility of supplying cover. They carried revolvers, because there were too many people close at hand for rifles; a shot from a rifle could travel half a mile, the distance to the highway.

The agents were dressed in black. The helicopters turned off their lights. Other agents watched the progress of the assault through night-vision glasses. The Highway Patrol team took possession of the barn floor. As the man prepared to raise the grappling hook toward the hay bales, one of the men carrying mirrors saw blood dripping through the floor of the loft. He raised his mirror, then climbed the ladder and peered into the loft and became the first person to lay close eyes on Mike Jackson in eleven days. He said, "It's over. He's dead."

JR Buchanan watched the procession of the night's activities—the helicopters, the talk, the dog, the tear gas, the assault—from the field between the house and the barn. When it ended he walked to the barn and climbed into the loft and took a long look at Mike's shoes. An agent knelt beside Mike. He lifted Mike's right hand carefully and in a way that appeared oddly tender and pressed an ink pad and then a piece of plain white paper against his thumb. Then he stood up, and, while a trooper beside him held a lamp, he looked, through a lens, back and forth between Mike's print and the copy from the files of the bureau. Perhaps a minute passed before he said, "Got it, got positive, it's him." Another agent called the command post over a radio.

"Ralph has made a positive," he said. "It is. The decedent. Mike. Wayne. Jackson."

"Ten-four. CP understands positive ID."

"Ten-four. Positive ID."

At the command post an agent came out of the office and into the large, low-ceilinged room that served as a dining hall. He held a radio above his head so that everyone— agents, troopers, and the people from the church—could hear what was being said at the barn. Through windows

opening onto the street, the reporters and townspeople waiting heard applause and weren't sure what to make of it.
Then some people joined hands and said a prayer.

Mike lay on his back. He had lost so much weight and
his features were so drawn that he had come to look like a
pilgrim. His head rested on some cotton ticking he had
found. Beneath his back was the blue coat. A white bedspread covered him nearly to the waist. He was wearing a
dark green shirt with a pattern to it and bluejeans—the
clothes he had on when he left Indianapolis. Somewhere he
had found a length of telephone cord and had tied one end
around the barrel of the shotgun and the other around the
stock as a strap. Before he lay down, he had taken off his
socks and laid them out to dry at his feet. Beside them he
had set his sneakers. He'd swept together some of the straw
to make a bed on the floor. At his left were five soybean
stalks gathered from the field where JR Buchanan had seen
his tracks, and to his right, just beyond the butt of the
shotgun, and the reach of his hand, a gallon milk jug filled
with water from the pond. His head rested on his left cheek.
His eyes were wide open and had something fanatical in
them, as if the last thing he had seen was a vision.

Before an audience of troopers and agents and firemen
and ambulance attendants, some of whom had an official
reason for being present and some of whom simply wanted
to stare at the man who had caused all this trouble, the
coroner unbuttoned Mike's shirt to look for a sign of what
happened to the bullet fired through the door of the Cadillac.
He found a small dent and decided Mike had received a
blow from something that broke his rib.

Just below Mike's right ear, the coroner found the circular

blue bruise—what is called a "tattoo"—where Mike had placed the barrel of the shotgun. Beneath the tattoo was the small patch of skin that had been covered by the hairs that were found in the sink of the trailer. The coroner pulled back the bedspread and saw Mike's bare feet. Stretched out on his back, with his long bony feet and the pallor of his skin, he looked like the corpse of a religious figure in a medieval painting. The coroner turned out Mike's pockets and found a plastic aspirin case, the kind sold at gas stations and convenience stores, empty, and a wadded-up, white cotton handkerchief.

They placed his body in a zippered bag brought to the loft by the funeral home director. The men standing around took the opportunity to look at him one last time. Then they closed the bag and lashed it to a stretcher and lowered Mike through a hole beside the ladder he had climbed by himself a few hours before.

His body spent the night in the back of a van in the garage at the funeral home. Meanwhile arrangements were made for an autopsy to be performed in St. Louis. Sometime during the night, the mortician and his assistant transferred Mike's body to a hearse so that the reporters waiting for the van to leave would not follow them. So much tear gas had been thrown into the barn that after the mortician placed Mike's body in the hearse he could still smell tear gas in the van. The hearse left Wright City just after dawn, with a Missouri State Highway Patrol car leading and another behind.

"When I got to the St. Louis University Medical Examiner's Office," says Doug Brown, the mortician, "they just took the body from me and said, 'Thank you,' and that was it, shut the door. I never seen them work so fast. Usually the morgue attendants will talk to you, say a few things, but this time, I guess with all the legal stuff around it, they were just all business."

After midnight, the man who distributed beer to Wright City and the country around opened his warehouse to the F.B.I. and the Highway Patrol and anyone else involved in the search, and some of the agents and troopers went by and had a beer, but most were too tired to stay and went back to their rooms in the motels, where they slept.

The celebration that people thought might take place never really came off, unless you count the few drivers who passed through town the next morning pressing on their horns. Relief at being delivered safely back to their regular lives is what most people felt. A teacher asked her children, "How many of you feel like they have had a ten-ton weight lifted?" and every small hand in the room rose toward the ceiling. Many people found themselves thinking about the figure of Modean, whose anguish they so plainly read in her manner on television, and that what the last week and a half had come down to in the end was not triumph so much as a frightened man putting a shotgun to his head in a barn in the dark far from home.

The next morning the agents had breakfast served to them at the command post by the women from the church. They filled out reports and used salt and pepper shakers and matchbooks and cigarette packs to re-create the layout of the buildings of the farm while they discussed what had happened. Then they boxed their papers and put them in the trunks of their cars and drove back to St. Louis. The woman who worked at city hall had her phones and her parking space back. Her assistant, the woman who had the doctor's note excusing her from the office, returned to work. The mayor sat back down at his desk and Chief Burgess sat at his.

Why didn't he run, is a question people put to themselves. Turn south from Wright City, place your back to the highway, you can go all the way to the Missouri River, fifteen miles, nothing but woods the whole way. Some people thought he was counting on the searchers to decide he was gone and fold the chase. Some thought that the small depression in the hay was proof he had been to the barn before, and that he had stayed close to the interstate in hopes of stealing a car from a traveller at the rest area. Or that the sound of traffic seemed to him a connection to the highway and escape. It did not make sense that he could have travelled two hundred fifty miles from Indianapolis, doing everything right, outthinking his pursuers, disappearing across Illinois, and leaving them wondering toward which point of the compass he had turned, and then hit their town and begun to behave like a man who could think of no alternatives.

People tried to imagine what went through his mind at the end. Some thought he was asleep and woke in a panic at the approach of the searchers and shot himself rather than be taken back to prison. Others thought the tidiness of the loft—his shoes carefully set beside his socks carefully stretched out to dry—and the odd, funereal aspect of his bare feet, showed he intended the loft to be the place where he made his last stand. Some considered his suicide an act of contrition. They pointed out that he had harmed no one but himself over the last eleven days, even though he must have had opportunities, and that as violently as his rampage had begun he apparently by the end only wanted to hide. Perhaps he had been brought to God. Eleven days of little food or water or shelter or sleep, with it raining nearly all the time and the ground turned to mud, and the constant threat of capture and the sound of dogs and helicopters in his ears and his having the opportunity to sit in the darkness and think of what he had done might be enough to convince a man that God was his only refuge. Or it might make him feel sufficiently cursed, harmed, and abandoned to turn a gun on himself and pull the trigger.

About fifty people watched his casket lowered to his grave in a cemetery in Memphis where Modean had bought a plot when she and Mike's father lived nearby. The casket was white, with gold details and brass fittings. A bouquet of red roses had lain on top of it at the funeral home. Modean leaned against it an enlargement of a black-and-white photograph taken in a studio of Mike when he was twelve or thirteen. He was smiling and wearing a white shirt and a bow tie and a jacket. The service at the grave lasted half an hour. The minister who presided came from Modean's church in Mississippi. "No one has done only good," he said, "and no one has done only evil."

It was believed in Wright City that Mike killed himself with the last shell that he had, but the afternoon he was buried, the Missouri State Highway Patrol checked the pockets of his coat and found nine shells, four dollars and sixty-two cents, and three gold rings.

PEOPLE IN WRIGHT CITY found it difficult to return to their lives. "When the manhunt ended," says Joy Strick, "it was like, 'What do we do now? Do I go back to washing clothes and making beds?' It was like there wasn't nothing important to do anymore."

Some people continued to sleep with their guns. Others tore down outbuildings that struck them as places where someone could hide. Instead of opening their windows on warm nights for a breeze, a lot of people locked them and slept with the air-conditioner on. They lost interest in walking through the woods. Looking out at the darkness, or taking the path toward their barns in the morning, or coming home at night to houses with the lights off, they found themselves more unsettled than they expected to be.

"It's a fear-paranoia-type situation," says Cookie Stude, "and when it's over, it's not over. It stays with you. I know when I drive out the highway there, through certain parts, past the farmhouse, it comes back to me: he was here. One of the F.B.I. agents when we sat down the next morning at the command post to serve rolls and coffee had this paper bag on the floor, and I looked at it, and it had a big red stain on the side of it, and he had some of Jackson's things in there, and I just turned aside. And I mean, I'm also an R.N., but that shook me. I just put it in a closet in my mind and shut the door, and I have never really been able to face it since. Sometimes I see that door opening, and I see that red spot, and I just close it up again. You don't like to hide your head in the sand, but it's hard. It leaves a mark. The fear doesn't really leave you. When you live in a small town and you know the policeman, and the mortician, and the men who picked up the body, you keep having associations in your mind. You see the location. And after, I don't think you ever feel the same way about things again."

Some people had real trouble recovering their lives. Their difficulties persisted. A connection seemed to have been severed, or a change had been made in their minds, and they weren't really sure how to get things back to the way they'd been before.

"We were in the kitchen area there at the command post," a woman recalls, "and I guess it was about eleven-thirty and the door to the headquarters office opened and one of the F.B.I. men came out and told us that it was over, that Mike had shot himself and everyone began to applaud—it wasn't that they were happy, just glad that it was over and that no one else had been hurt—and it was like a switch had been turned on inside me, because I just somehow felt that I was feeling something different about this from anyone else. It was like I had suddenly stepped outside of myself and didn't know how to get back in. And my heart was pounding and I felt as if everyone could tell.

"I thought in the weeks to come that I was handling it fine. I didn't go to any of the support groups they were having, I just didn't think I needed it, and by the time I realized I did, they were finished. I started collecting newspaper articles. What triggered it, I guess, was when everyone started getting their pictures back, and I got interested in having copies and in collecting the articles and I began to assemble them into a scrapbook because that seemed like the only thing I had any interest in doing and also because I was trying to figure out what had happened, what there was in the experience of the manhunt that had led me to feeling this way.

"Around January of 1987, I guess, is when I started putting the articles in scrapbooks and lettering captions for them. In February I made a trip to Indianapolis, where I have relatives, but I also knew in some part of my mind that I would go to the library and get the articles from the Indianapolis papers about the case.

"In the meantime I was also just talking about the case constantly and of course I couldn't help but notice that not everyone had the same interest in doing so that I did. Some people treated it like it was some kind of thing that had happened and now it was over and you never talked about it again. Like a tornado had come through and you rebuilt and never mentioned the subject. I don't know exactly what there was about the experience of those days—I mean, I wasn't seized by the figure of Jackson, or the mysteries of the case, why he had done what he had, or where he had lain at night, or where he had travelled over those eleven days, or whether I had come near him—but there was just some comfort in the idea of raising the subject and there were certain people with whom I could reminisce for hours. We'd start talking and one of us would say, do you remember when this or that happened, or about some person. Everyone in the kitchen effort I think became attached to one or two people from the search, took an interest in them, and made friendships, some of which they've kept up. As there were no more articles about the manhunt after a while, I began over the years to collect articles about people I'd known who'd been involved. The agent who'd been a part of one of the tactical teams and was later killed in St. Louis. Hal Helterhoff when he was transferred to Detroit.

"Eventually I decided I needed psychological help and it took me a while to find the right person and then I did and worked through it with him for two years until the spring of 1990. I haven't really looked at the scrapbooks in a year, but things still come up and I add to them, and every time I do I hope it is the last time. I don't think any-one who didn't live through it can understand what it was like."

FOR SOME PEOPLE the experience wasn't over until they had been to the barn and climbed into the loft and stared at the bloody hay and the pieces of Jackson's brain that the coroner left behind on the walls. A picture of the loft is pasted to the pages of a lot of photograph albums in Wright City. Hundreds of people came to the barn. They retraced Mike's steps and stood there feeling his presence and said things like, "It sure is strange," or, "It's eerie standing here," if they said anything at all, and when they left they often took pieces of the barn with them.

During the manhunt an elderly woman named Margaret Lange heard a voice in her dreams telling her to write to Mike's mother. She woke in the morning and said, "But, Lord, I don't know where to write." After she heard the instruction on three nights, over the course of a month, she put some scriptures in an envelope and sent them to Modean in Oxford, Mississippi, where the papers said she lived, and wrote on the envelope, "Lord, please deliver." She mailed the envelope late on a Thursday and on Sat-urday morning her phone rang. "You don't know what a blessing it was," said Modean, "to get your letter with the scripture."

The barn no longer exists. It was torched a few days before the Halloween of the year after the manhunt. One of the teachers at school had been thinking of using it for a haunted house. No one knows who burned it. Some people say it was set on fire by the owners, who were tired of the insurance risk involved in having people crawl all over their property. Barn-burning is a pretty common activity in that part of Missouri, though, and Chief Burgess thinks some kids set it ablaze for a thrill. The walls caved in and the roof fell and the metal twisted in the fire. Where it stood has grown up into pokeweed and goldenrod and horseweed and mare's tail and daisy fleabane. How Modean came to have a photograph of the barn is that Margaret Lange stood far enough back in the field to frame the whole of the structure in her lens. On the back of the photograph, Modean wrote, " 'Barn of Darkness' Loft. I prayed that night for Mike. I believe God took him 'To the Father's Mansion Prepared for him.' "

CITIZENS:

"He was here to visit his wife and young'uns. He's got young'uns in this country and he was coming *home*! That's what I heard."

"Jimmy Taylor says Jackson crossed his brother's property one night. Said the dog barked, and that old dog don't bark for just nothing, now."

"Cary Watson says he got up one morning, six a.m., opened his door and saw Jackson standing in his field."

First citizen: "What's that road out there where they work on trucks and it's got that parts store . . . ?"

Second: "I don't know the name of those roads. Never did."

Third: "*Fruit* Farm Road."

First: "No, that ain't it. Out there by those bean fields.

Leo, that road cross the country there where it's all netted up, you got to slow down when you come to the crossing?"

Third: "Fruit Farm Road!"

First: "No, that ain't it. That's it if you're driving from the other direction."

Second: "Leon Taylor lives out that way, but I can't tell you the name of it."

First: "Well, I don't know, but I heard someone out there say they thought they saw him running over the fields and into the woods plain as daylight."

"Wes said Jackson smacked his dog. They heard it yelping. Cornered it up against a fence and he smacked it."

First citizen: "I heard Lonnie Price say he heard that shot. What was it, about four? . . . Six-*thirty*? Well, see, I've forgotten some of it already. He said he heard that shot, you know, that *pop*, said he heard that out across the fields up at his place."

Second: "Well, where's Lonnie live? Out across the highway, right?"

First: "Yeah, back up there."

Second: "Well, how's he going to hear that shot, far away as he is? He didn't hear no shot."

First: "Well, I don't know. I didn't ask him, but somebody told me, 'Lonnie, now, he heard that shot.' "

"Those two elderly ladies up there, sisters, which they're twins. I heard they saw him. Didn't say day or night, just that they had."

"Lyle Davis says Jackson was standing one night on the back steps of the funeral home. Not the old one. The new one they got fixed up now. On the back steps like a statue with the light shining on him."

First citizen: "He was so far away from home. I wonder what he was doing down here."

Second: "Getting away."

First: "Getting away, I guess. I guess he was just getting away."

THE TURNING WHEEL

TOM HAD BEEN BURIED several months when Nancy first went to his grave. It was a cold, windy day, and it was raining. She had expected to remember the location of the plot, but when she got to the cemetery she realized that she had found it on the day of the funeral because a tent was set up and everyone was already standing beside it. She followed a map she was given at the cemetery's office, but when she got to the site she found two graves side by side, with nothing to identify whose they were. She stood in the rain, crying and studying the map and the graves for any indication of the one in which her husband lay. A man digging a grave nearby came to help her. She asked which grave was Tom Gahl's, and he said, "Was he the lawyer?" She told him who he was, and the gravedigger pointed to the grave. He said he knew which grave belonged to the probation officer because so many people had asked him directions to it. Sometimes when Nancy visits the grave she finds flowers. On this occasion, she brought Tom a rose.

She bought a headstone and had the engraver inscribe it "Jesus Loved Thee Best." Only later did she realize that the phrase allowed a prideful interpretation. It pained her to think that some people might regard the inscription as arrogant.

Nancy finds it difficult to visit Tom's grave. All the ways that he lives within her dissolve when confronted by the mound where his body lies. The boys approach the grave slowly, with their eyes averted, and leave it as soon as they can. In the cemetery they are reminded of what they have suffered and no longer have, and lose hold of the loving image they nurture in their minds and hearts.

Early in her first winter as a widow Nancy dreamed she was standing in a room and Tom came in and hugged her. The sensation of having his arms around her was powerful enough that, waking, she had an almost physical memory of the embrace.

She discovered a laundry bag she'd forgotten about that had in it clothes to which the scent of her husband still clung. She would raise them to her face and draw deep breaths and collect from them what comfort she could, until, over time, the scent was eclipsed by the scent of the cloth.

Some of her friends thought Nancy would put the house on the market, but too many things in it reminded her of Tom and she had no wish to sever what little connection was left. Also she felt that Nicholas and Christopher would need their lives as little changed as possible. She imagined that it must seem to them as if the world had spun out of control. She hoped that the house would provide some ground on which they might find rest and stability and feel safe.

The boys began to have trouble falling asleep. Their minds

would race as they lay in the dark and the only thing that soothed them was to talk to their mother. Christopher worried that someone would break into the house as they slept and kill them. Nancy told him she would do everything she could to protect them, which helped, except that sometimes after she left the room Christopher fell to wondering exactly what his mother could do against an intruder, especially a madman. It became a kind of balancing act he had to perform, to hold on to the comfort of his mother's words while not letting his mind drift too far toward considering them.

Night after night, lying in their beds with their mother sitting beside them, the boys would need to hear that nothing they might have done could have prevented their father's being murdered. Perhaps if one of them had been sick that morning, their father might not have gone to work. Maybe they should have asked for a ride to school, or said something at breakfast to delay him. They knew he had walked or run past his car in trying to escape from Jackson, and they wonder why he hadn't got in it and driven away. They knew that every time they saw a scene in a movie or on television where a villain menaced an innocent person, someone showed up and shot him, or knocked the gun from his hand as he fired, and they wondered why that hadn't happened when it mattered so much.

Christopher was particularly troubled by the thought that his lingering in the bathroom the morning of the murder meant that his father had pulled away from the house without seeing him wave from the driveway. He would ask Nancy whether she thought that his father had driven away thinking that he was staring at himself in the mirror, instead of saying farewell, and she would say she was sure that his father had seen him.

Christopher began to require that all the windows in his room be shut once darkness fell. No matter how hot it became in the room, he was unable to sleep with them open. Nicholas began also to insist his windows be closed. Sometimes Nancy was able to persuade him to open them by saying she would close them when she came up to bed. If she happened to notice that one of the boys was experimenting with having a window open and mentioned that it represented progress, the window would immediately be closed and locked. Often when she kissed the boys good night, their rooms were sweltering and the sheets were damp.

Addressing their fears in the way that she might have before the murder—that is, by telling them not to worry, that they were safe in their home—no longer answered. "You can't tell them not to worry," she says, "that they have nothing to fear, that nothing can happen, because they already know what *has* happened." The prison picture of Jackson that appeared every day on television and in the papers was one that both Christopher and Nicholas found themselves able to conjure without trying. More often, it appeared as a visitation. They were now able to invoke the figure and face of the demon in their closets or under their beds. Christopher began to wake in the night and see Jackson's face within the frame of his window. The expression it wore made him feel that Jackson was gloating at having cornered him.

For months after the murder Nancy would wake early. She would occupy her mind until five minutes past eight and then she would think, This is when Tom got shot. She began to note the arrival of the time on significant days, five past eight on the morning of the Monday one month after the murder, two months after, and so on. "It seemed like such a dark time," she says. "I remember thinking I was in for a cold, cold winter and wishing that I could just make it through till spring."

One way that she tried to make peace with the horror of the murder was to imagine Heaven as a place where Tom found rest. She thought no more about it than that; during the first six months after he'd been shot it was triumph enough to make it from one day to the next. After six months passed, the idea was borne in on her that if Tom was at peace he wasn't aware of the pain that she and the boys were suffering over his loss. If he wasn't aware of it, he couldn't be watching, and he could no longer be caring for them, either. That there was no connection between him and them anymore was another blow she was forced to accept.

People frequently asked if she had any experiences of being in a room where a chair moved suddenly without explanation, or of feeling a draft when no window was open, or any sense at all of Tom's sending messages from the spirit world. She knows that people report experiences of this kind all the time, but she thinks that perhaps she may not have felt anything like it because she imagined Tom as arriving immediately in Heaven, not as lingering.

The course of her grief was unpredictable but relentless. It seemed that it would go on forever. The place she selected to receive what she thought of as its "deepest, most convulsive, and drowning aspects" was the bedroom, and the occasions were days when the boys were at school. She felt that whatever recovery she might hope for lay in the direction of enduring all that the ordeal demanded. What confronted her appeared enormous and not to have any outline, so it seemed the only way to address it was by means of one memory at a time. It was as if her memories were part of a turning wheel that brought each to the surface for a time, then submerged it, while another took its place, and so on, until the wheel had come full circle and she was back where she had started. A friend of hers told her to concentrate her mind on thinking upward, toward light, toward the sky and toward heaven, but Nancy often found herself in the depths without knowing how she got there. What scared her was that she had no idea how deep her grief could be. As intense or painful as her experience of it was, she never felt she came to the bottom of it. To protect herself from disappearing into it, she would occasionally have to put parts of it aside until she felt strong enough to consider them. There were mornings when she would wake and try immediately to think of something to engage her mind and keep it from straying toward whatever had disturbed her the night before.

For a year she found it difficult to shake the picture of the murder she held in her mind. At moments when she was tired or not thinking of anything in particular, the image presented itself with an insistence that made her feel "like I was being dragged back to Tom in that pool of blood." The agent from the F.B.I. had told her the lapse of time between the first shot and the second, which killed Tom, was about a minute. But still, she would think, that last minute. As many times as she replayed the scene in her mind, it always ended the same—nothing she could do to interrupt it, no comfort she could bring him. How she finally got through the experience was by imagining Tom not as she recalled him but as a figure ahead of her in Heaven with whom she might hope to be reunited. The complication it introduced was that Tom became a figure she could locate in the past and the future, but one who was invisible in the present.

The pull toward the past had a life of its own. "Something happens that you don't expect," she says. "You hear a song on the radio, or open a drawer and see a shirt he wore, or someone makes a gesture that reminds you of Tom, even though the person doesn't look anything like him, or an image comes to your mind from something you see in a landscape as you pass in your car, and it opens the whole thing up."

On the first anniversary of her wedding that followed the murder, she sat on her bed and looked through the pictures of her and Tom, the party, the family, the cake, the tables, the linens, the dance, and wept over each one.

She thought often of all she would never do with him again. She remembered making love. She recalled the pleasure of talking at the end of the day. "We always talked things through," she says. "Neither of us liked to brood, and when it finally dawns on you that you will never have those conversations—the ones with the person who knows everything about your life, and who you mean when you refer to this or that person and what they mean to you and what your history with them is, conversations with someone who understands you so completely and deeply—when you realize that is gone, then it is like something has been taken from you that you can never recover."

A FEW MONTHS after his father was murdered, Christopher asked his mother what his father's voice sounded like.

"I really can't remember," he said. It pained her that the memory Christopher had of his father was turning elusive. She has worked to keep the boys' memories of him alive. It concerns her that sometimes she probably forces them to recall him for reasons of her own, because it wounds her that they can't. Or because she needs to feel him revived. Or because she is aware of all the things their father could have helped them with and that she feels unprepared by her experience for: how to instruct Christopher in the way to put on his football equipment, how to teach them to knot a necktie, saw a board, hammer a nail, throw a football. The point of her concern of course being how will they receive an introduction to all the mysteries of masculinity that a loving father would have given them, small rituals like shaving, or how to cast a fishing rod, or to operate a piece of machinery, lessons that can pass as important moments of intimacy between a father and son, where a child gets a piece of information in the context of weakness protected by strength, then learns to use it himself and grows strong. She wonders whether the boys will experience the sense of a father standing above them, then beside them as they grow, his eyes looking into their own, or the sense of a father turning from them and the sight of his back as he leaves.

DURING THE WINTER following the murder it occurred to Nancy that while she had got back Tom's wedding ring and his wallet and his briefcase, no one had returned his clothes. The police department didn't know where they were. Someone in the probation department knew the chief of police and called him, and the clothes were turned up in a property room. The officer who called Nancy said, "Are you sure you want them?"

A detective brought the clothes to the house in a box. "I don't know what I was expecting," Nancy says, "but they were all crumpled up, and there was dried blood everywhere that had dried hard, so it was like starch had been put on them, and they were just this big crusty ball in a box, and the box had holes punched in it for air, and there were dead flies in it.

"I washed them and that was so hard. To look in the machine—the water was just red, a reddish black—and see all of his blood."

A day at a time, she made it through the winter. During the spring the event that came to dominate her mind was the approach of the first anniversary of the murder. When the day arrived she went to the house where Jackson had lived. A friend went with her. When the friend arrived to pick her up, around eight-thirty that morning, Nancy said to her, "Tom was already dead." Nancy stood at the intersection of Orange Street and Pleasant Run Parkway and witnessed the scene in the eye of her mind as she had done thousands of times in the year before, only this time the image came to her more clearly. She did not have to invent the setting—it was right there before her—and she could concentrate on details. "I knew that he had left the house at twenty to eight," she says, "and got to Jackson's at eight and was dead at five after and the Grape-Nuts he had for breakfast were still in his stomach, so this time, standing there at the house, on the sidewalk where he lay and looking back at the house and the walk they must have travelled together, I really knew what had happened. When it happened for real I didn't know until four hours later."

She left a rose on a low stone wall that had appeared behind Tom in the background of all the photographs in the papers.

She went to church, then toured a hospital on the advice of a friend who knew that Nancy was considering volunteer work and thought she might find something to engage herself there. In the afternoon she went back to the house with her father and Nicholas and Christopher. They noticed that someone had cleared out the tangle of brush and carpenters had put up new siding, so it no longer looked as frightening as it had in the papers. Nancy hoped that seeing it might partly relieve the sense the boys had of a madman living in a haunted house. Nicholas and Christopher wondered if they would see the stain of their father's blood on the sidewalk. Nicholas, who was five, found a coin on the ground and thought maybe it had come from his father's pocket.

It was a fine fall day. In the air was a certain sharpness which Nancy thinks of as being a part of that time of year. It had been in the air the day Tom died, and it clenched her heart to feel it again.

The phone rang at the end of the day and a voice said, "This is Carolyn," and she gave her last name, and then she said, "I was married to Mike Jackson." No one where she worked knew her past, so she hadn't felt able to talk about the thoughts she was having. She suggested that she and Nancy meet sometime for coffee. She was sure that if they did, Nancy would never think of her as the kind of woman to have been married to Mike Jackson. Nancy was too surprised by her call to make much of a reply. They made no date to meet, and never have. When she hung up Nancy felt interested, but also alarmed.

A woman called who was part of the crew of the ambulance that removed Tom's body from the street. She told Nancy that she had never seen a body so damaged. She said that the experience caused her to quit her job and find other work. For some reason she felt it proper to tell Nancy this.

ELEVEN DAYS LATER, on the anniversary of Mike's death, Nancy sent Modean a rose. She had thought of her alone with her sorrow. Modean called that night. She told Nancy that she had carried the rose with her to a church meeting that evening and that when she told people who had sent it, no one could believe it.

A few months later, around Christmas of 1987, Modean sat in the living room of Nancy's house. She had called and asked if she could visit and Nancy agreed, hoping that the figure of an elderly woman might ease for the boys their terror of the man who murdered their father. Modean brought Oneita. She also gave Nicholas and Christopher a small picture in a frame of two farm boys which Nancy believes she got at a K mart, or someplace like it. Modean opened her purse and handed them photographs of Mike. In one he stands in a backyard facing the camera, with picnic benches behind him. He is wearing a coat and tie and has short hair and no beard and his posture is that of the obedient, solid citizen—a high school teacher, perhaps—except that the tense, sad, and troubled expression on his face suggests a mental patient on a weekend pass. Nancy was aware that Modean expected the pictures to alter how she felt about Jackson, but they moved her not at all. What she remembers Modean and Oneita saying most often was that God would take care of her and the boys.

The boys sat without speaking. They examined the pictures they were shown without taking them in their hands. Modean and Oneita spoke of Mike sentimentally, as if he had become a different person in death. Nancy was made uncomfortable by the discordance between the tone of their recollections and the feeling they gave her of being relieved at Mike's having come to his end. The truth, she felt, was that no one knew what to do with such a man when he was living, and that it was easier to think warmly of him when he no longer menaced their lives. Nancy did not feel they weren't entitled to think of him in a kind of cleaned-up, after-death way, but it startled her to hear Modean talk as if some thread of Nancy's and the boys' experience was common to her and Oneita's. Modean seemed to be suggesting that because she and Oneita had lost a son and a brother and Nancy had lost her husband and the boys their father, their losses put them all on the same ground.

Oneita took some pictures of Modean with Nancy and the boys. When they left, Nicholas and Christopher wanted to know why she had come. Christopher held out the picture of the farm boys and said, "What is this?" and his voice nearly cracked, he was so angry. He and Nicholas destroyed the picture.

"After that," Nancy says, "Modean sent me a letter and it said, 'God will take care of you,' and she enclosed a tape of her preacher delivering a sermon. I wrote back and thanked her, and then she sent more tapes, and they weren't really that helpful to me—they were Born-Again Fundamentalist preaching—so I wrote back and thanked her and said that it wasn't really necessary to send any more—that I had my own spiritual help.

"I suppose it went farther than I wanted it to. She was

always writing how her family was so normal and close, and there wasn't any way really that that would mean anything to me. She even sent more pictures of Jackson, but I think I threw them out. I was afraid Christopher would find them and be angry. At some point I wrote her, politely, because I just had to let her know that our lives were different from hers, and I think what I said was, 'The pain will never end.'"

She tells the story with no trace of outrage.

Not long after the visit from Oneita and Modean, Nancy and one of her brothers and the boys were driving to Topeka. As they approached Wright City, she didn't tell the boys where they were, but she said she had to make a stop. They left the highway, and as they pulled into town they saw a sheriff's car parked with a deputy in it. Her brother rolled down the window and told the deputy that they wanted to see the barn where Mike Jackson died. "My sister was one of his victims," he said. The deputy said, "If you're one of his victims, then we have something in common," and it turned out that he was the deputy Jackson had shot. The boys were upset when they realized where they were, but decided that they wanted to go through with it. He took them to the farmhouse. The barn had already burned, but he showed them where it had stood, and then he showed them the structure on the property that most closely resembled it. Then he took them into town to meet the mayor and see city hall, where they noticed the poster of Jackson on the wall.

UNEXPECTEDLY, the second year of widowhood was harder than the first. "I don't tell that to any of my widow friends," she says. She had stood where Tom fell partly from love, partly from an intuition that doing so was proper, and partly from a kind of magic-thinking which held that a just and unflinching observance of his death might lift some of the burden that lay on her heart. When she woke the next morning and felt no different, she thought she had accomplished nothing.

"Your whole life," she says, "you are taught to believe that when you work for something, there is a reward at the end. You work hard the first year trying to recover, then the second arrives and you realize that with grieving there is no accomplishment; things will never change, nor will they ever again be the same. There is no reward. There's nothing at the end. Your loss is permanent."

What she noticed in the second year was that any occasion of significance was separated by one degree from the last she shared with Tom. During her first year alone she could recollect her last wedding anniversary, and recall that Tom had been there, or the last passing of the boys' birthdays, and remember what she and Tom had done to mark them. During the second year she began to feel as if a hole had opened up between her and her husband.

The boys began to form questions they kept asking for years. They wondered whether they might be more scared at night if their father had survived the shooting—if his presence, more than his absence, would call to their minds the terrors and violence of the world. They wondered whether the first shot had severed their father's arm, whether it lay beside him on the ground, and whether, if he had survived, he would have learned to throw a ball with his other arm. They wondered if he could have survived the second shot had there not been a third. What color was Jackson's truck? they would ask Nancy. What happened to their father's brain? Was it simply left lying in the road? Was there anything left to the part of his head that lay beneath the shroud in the casket?

Christopher's mind is sometimes engaged in spite of himself. He wonders if his father and Jackson talked first and there was an argument and Jackson lost his temper. Did Jackson only mean to rob his father and take his car? Where did Jackson stand, and where was his father? What was the expression on Jackson's face? What made him pull the trigger? And what happened after that? Sometimes he wonders what his father's last words were. On occasion he says to his mother, "I want to meet those witnesses." Trying to take in the enormity of what happened, the boys find themselves overwhelmed by the details. They ask the same questions over and over, as if they had never heard the answers, but it is a ritual. Each time they come closer to absorbing the truth.

Christopher knows that pictures were made by the police of his father lying dead in the street, and there are times he wants to look at them, but he worries that the shock of seeing them will make him go crazy and that he will stay that way for the rest of his life.

Nancy sometimes also feels a need to see the pictures. She felt it often and strongly the first and second years following his murder. After that the need appeared to go away, then returned. There are times when it is all she can do not to try and track down copies, and times when it doesn't matter to her at all. She wonders whether she is punishing herself by giving way to the need to experience all she can of Tom's end. It has occurred to her that the desire might represent a need to seek a connection with her husband by any means she can. Any evidence he was here might somehow offer a way of finding the door back to before all this happened and the chance to prevent its taking place. Or also its opposite: to come finally to terms with the loss in such a way that one's life can go forward, without being pulled constantly into the past.

Nancy is subject to night fears. When Tom was alive she would sometimes reach for his hand in the darkness. She would listen to his breathing.

She always told Tom he was going to outlive her. She expected to die early, as her mother had. She told Tom he would have to live longer because the boys needed their father.

One night, in the second year after the murder, Christopher dreamed that his father stood at the end of his bed, wounded and bleeding, and called his name. Then he fell forward onto the bed.

ABOUT A YEAR after Modean came to her house, Nancy received a call from Jimmy Jackson, asking if he could come and see her. He said he had something to help the boys, but he didn't say what it was. "I didn't figure he would want to hurt me," she says, "because Modean gave him my number, and I didn't think she would do anything further to harm us.

"The doorbell rang, and he came in with another man and sat at the table in the dining room and the other man sat with him. He spread a folder out on the table, and said he was getting into a new line of business. Ordinarily, he was a truck driver, but what he wanted was to sell me a plan of some kind for investing my money. The man with him was someone he was training with, or maybe someone he went to church with, I can't recall. As I sat there looking at the structure of his face it kept going through my mind that his brother must have looked something like him; I kept thinking, so that's what Mike Jackson looked like, and that's the last person Tom saw. I guess when I recovered myself I told him we were already taken care of and didn't need anything additional.

"As they were leaving I asked Jimmy if he was the brother who had wanted to see Mike Jackson in his casket—Modean had told me that one of them had—and he just said something about how it was an unfortunate thing, and that was all; he just wanted to get out the door. But I wanted to know something for myself from all of this. I listened to him and now I wanted to see if I could learn anything that would help me. But I didn't. Toward the end it seemed to dawn on the other man who I was.

"What Jimmy was thinking I have no idea. Perhaps it was his way of setting something right, a gesture."

A few months later a letter arrived, the address written in Modean's hand. In the envelope, an invitation for Christopher, Nancy, and Nicholas to a reunion of Mike's family.

THE DAYS of the second year passed. Nancy would pray sometimes as she lay awake in the middle of the night not to be tested any further and to be allowed to live out her life and raise her children. What she hoped for, to see them through, was another twenty years. "If some accident were to befall me and these boys be without a mother," she says,

"I don't know what would happen. They would have other people who would care for them and love them, but no one who would love them like a mother. And if I were to lose one of them, I don't know how I would survive it. They say the Lord doesn't give you more than you can handle, but if that were to happen I think it would be more than I could bear. My younger son said that if something happened to me he didn't know if he could believe there really was a God."

It is difficult to give Christopher and Nicholas an explanation of how their father, who (apparently) harmed no one, who (as far as anyone knows) went about the business of caring and providing for his family as truthfully and benevolently as he was able, who seemed to ask no more from the world than safe passage for him and the people he loved, could come early to death, on a fine, sunny morning, on a street in front of other people, at the hands of a man who pointed a shotgun at his eyes. The only explanation she has been able to give them is that Jackson was crazy, sick, disordered, a criminal not acting like a normal person. For the boys this explanation has meant that the world has come to seem chaotic and menacing and disordered itself, and that anything terrible and violent can happen at any time. Nicholas sometimes prays that nothing violent happens to them anymore, but that if it does, it should take all of them at once.

To protect himself from the desolation he sometimes feels when the subject of his father comes up, Christopher occasionally falls back on a defense of amnesia. If he feels his mother has become too insistent on his recalling a memory that causes him discomfort he will sometimes tell her that he has no idea what she could possibly be referring to. He will say sometimes that he cannot remember his father at all. When this happens, Nancy lets the matter drop. She knows Christopher will come to her later and tell her he knew precisely what she was talking about, that he remembers the dream in which his father appeared as a corpse, say, but that he has worked hard to put it out of his mind and recover, and now that it has come up he doesn't know if he can ever be happy again. It is as if a whirlpool or a maelstrom occupied the territory engaged by his father in his mind, and for him to go near it is dangerous. Sometimes it feels as if the memory of his father lies at the bottom of an abyss in his mind and that now and then he goes to the edge and looks down at it, then recoils. It is a test he is constantly setting himself.

When he is feeling overwhelmed he will say that what he can remember of his father's funeral are the presents that arrived for him and his brother, the food and the flowers and the people being around and then gone, and returning to school with everyone knowing what had happened, but that is all. He sometimes thinks that what happened to him in losing his father sounds so removed from the ordinary life of a child that it is as if it were something he read about a boy in a story set a long time ago.

THE IMAGE of their father the boys held in their minds grew harder to summon as they got older. When Nicholas thinks of his father he tends to recall him as he appears in a photograph and not as he knew him. The photograph he sees in his mind is not perfectly focused. It is stationary and fixed in time. It has suffered no change, got no older. Whereas the photograph served when his father was alive as a reference for the warmth and benevolence he felt from his father, the image has become enigmatic and aloof, as if the person it depicts wouldn't quite be able to remember who Nicholas was. Where it once captured a moment in the life of his father, it has come to stand for nearly all moments. Once it was a fraction of the image of his father—his father in a particular mood, at a particular moment. Now it is the total. His father has remained in the past, rooted in time and place but adrift in the child's memory. More and more, his father occupies a position on a landscape that is not exactly a dream, but doesn't seem real either. A child asked to think of his father is likely to summon an image of him as he appears in the present. Nicholas responds no differently, except that the most prominent likeness of his father in the present is the picture of him hanging on the wall above his bed.

THEY CAN still see the wallpaper he hung in the hall and the mantel he built over the fireplace where there hasn't been a fire since he died. If they open a closet in their mother's bedroom they can try on his clothes. In the garage they can hammer nails or turn screws with his tools. At the edge of the yard they can shoot baskets through the net he hung. They walk through the same door he did, climb the same stairs, sit at the same table, drink from the same glasses, eat from the same plates, use the same knives and forks, but he is no longer their first association to these objects or actions. It is to be expected that his image would grow less distinct in their minds as they age. They have changed and he hasn't. In recalling him they are constantly re-creating him, each time differently. It is not likely that each recalls in the same way the man whose image appears in the photograph, their experiences of him, and their ages, being different. Not long ago Christopher told his mother that he was starting to feel as if he never had a father. Nancy knows that the memories Christopher and Nicholas have lose their intensity and are replaced and that sometimes the replacements are not factual but are ones she has given them, or that they have reconstructed for themselves. The further they move from the presence of their father, the less certain of their memories they can be. He becomes less who he was and more who they need him to be, or would like him to have been, or need him to have been. It is not that the image they summon is no longer intact, only more unpredictable.

THE BOYS GREW RELUCTANT to spend the night away from home. They did not care to be separated from their mother, or to trust the dark in someone else's house. In addition, they feared something happening to Nancy while they were away. Christopher felt that if any harm came to his mother while he wasn't there to protect her, he could never forgive himself. He also feared what might happen to him and his brother if they found themselves orphaned. Feeling that the boys would know better than anyone else when they were ready, Nancy did not force them. In calming their anxieties about being safe at night in their beds, Nancy would say, "Our house has always been safe, Daddy was killed away from home when he was at work, and I'm here to protect you." But that only made it more difficult for them to face being away.

Neither boy likes to be left alone either upstairs or down at night. If one is in the shower upstairs and the other leaves the floor, there is a quarrel afterward. For years Christopher would not go upstairs alone at night. Nor downstairs. Nicholas would, and could sometimes be persuaded to retrieve something Christopher left behind. He then accused Christopher of cowardice and of making him do his dirty work.

TOM'S FATHER DIED a few months before he did. On one of his trips to his mother's after his father was buried Tom brought back a birdhouse his father built. It needed repair and Tom set to work on it in the garage for no reason except that it had been assembled by his father. He hadn't made much progress on it when his own death arrived. It is still in the garage, beside the box that Tom's clothes came back from the morgue in. Nancy has not felt able to part with either the birdhouse or the cardboard box with the holes punched in it. She has only recently arrived at a point where she can consider giving up anything that reminds her of Tom. Occasionally her eye is startled by the sight of Christopher wearing a tie of his father's. Sometimes he wears his father's shirts.

Eventually she sold his car. A friend of their lawyer's handled it for them without taking any commission. On the morning of the day that Nancy delivered it to him, she and Nicholas and Christopher took turns sitting in the driver's seat and putting their hands on the wheel. Then the boys stood in front of it and had their pictures taken. They went off to school, and when they came home it was gone.

For four years Nancy changed nothing about the appearance of the house. The foundation sagged and had to be jacked up, and that alteration left the frame of the front door at an angle. Nancy let it stay that way, because it couldn't be fixed without removing the wallpaper in the front hall, which Tom had hung. Then, when four years had passed, she had her bedroom painted. It had been beige when she occupied it with Tom, and she had it painted white, with blue trim. She also installed a bay window in it overlooking the yard where the boys play. She knows the new room, which she thinks of as feminine, would not be one Tom would have felt comfortable in.

THE CLOTHES TOM WAS WEARING when he was killed are in the attic above the garage. A friend who works in the restoration department of a museum got for her bags and boxes of the kind in which museums store fabrics. The clothes are kept in the attic because Christopher didn't want them in the house; he was afraid they would remind him too vividly of his father's murder. During the spring when he was twelve—that is, four years after the murder—he heard his mother talking about them and asked if she would bring them out. She pulled down the folding stairs to the attic, then laid the clothes on the playroom table. The belt had the case number on it. Nancy said, "You can see where he was shot on his arm with the first shot and how he held it against his side, from all the blood." She ran her fingers over the holes the pellets had made in the collar and neck of the shirt. She asked Christopher how he felt seeing them. "It can't hurt me," he said, "because I don't remember him," and it was as if he had walked up to the abyss for a moment and stared straight in.

The sadness never goes away. Over the years the quality of her mourning has changed from inescapable grief born of her husband's sudden, thuggish removal from her life, to a persistent melancholy over living without him. Accepting, finally, that he lies in the cemetery does not prevent her from thinking, I wish he were here. It does not seem any longer that she is grieving but, rather, that she is facing the fact of her loss.

Her father suffered the early death of her mother, then married again. When she occasionally thinks she has endured all there is to be felt about Tom's death, she recalls her father's experience. "My father told me that he was fine for years, and then the twentieth anniversary of her death came around and he just fell apart. We talked on the phone and he was in tears. I think of it because in a few years coming up the anniversary of Tom's murder will be on a Monday again, and I am braced."

Friends now and then tell her she should see other men, but she doesn't know if she could. She wears her wedding ring. "I'm still married in my heart to this man," she says. Her feelings, however, are complicated beyond fidelity. "I can't imagine loving someone again," she says, "because it would mean going through this loss and grieving all over. I talk with my father about it, because by remarrying he realizes he's let himself in for it all over again. Another death to endure."

A situation that Nicholas and Christopher haven't had to experience is the sight of their mother in the company of another man. Nancy once gave a hug to a man who was a friend of the family as he was leaving the house and Christopher, watching them, said, "I wish Dad was here to see this." While she has no interest in seeing anyone, she knows that part of the reason is that she has the company of her children. Their being disinclined to stay away from home means that she has not felt lonely on weekends. For four and a half years after Tom died, Nancy spent only two Friday nights by herself. She knows this could change as Christopher gets older and starts to go out with girls.

For Christopher the presence of another man in the house disturbs the stillness that has settled in around the death of his father. The sameness of everything is a comfort. With so little having changed in the house there is the sense that his father could walk through the door as if he had only been on a trip that had required he stay away longer than he had planned. There is a feeling in the house that everything in it has been waiting for him since the day he left.

As the years passed, an aspect of Christopher's personality, a desire for order, intensified. Whenever he feels pressured, he begins to organize objects around him in rows and stacks and columns. Anything left on a counter by his mother or his brother goes into a drawer or a closet. Nancy tends to leave her mail on the table in the kitchen, and often he puts it away before she can go through it, and she doesn't find it again, so some bills go unpaid. Sometimes she takes food out of the refrigerator and goes upstairs for something and when she gets back Christopher has put the food away. Occasionally he shows up in the frame of her bedroom door and says, "What happened to your *room*?" Once when he came home and found Nancy in the kitchen talking to a man who was a family friend he began immediately to walk around the room opening drawers and putting whatever was on the counter into them. He is aware that he does it, and he and Nancy have struck an agreement that he can, so long as it does not become pronounced, and if it does they sit down and talk about what is bothering him.

In the garage hangs a punching bag bought at the suggestion of a psychologist to whom Christopher once made three visits. The psychologist was a former probation officer and saw Christopher at no charge. When Christopher feels the need to unburden himself he will use the bag.

IN A CLOSET off the kitchen Nancy keeps files that have in them relics of the case. Somewhere among them is the wanted poster of Jackson. Exactly where it is, she doesn't know. She hid it so Nicholas and Christopher wouldn't find it.

Four years after the murder, Christopher asked to see it. He wanted to hang it in his room, but Nancy was reluctant to look for it. She worried it would only frighten him. She had the feeling he was testing how much of the picture and the presence of Jackson he could tolerate, and she wasn't sure it was a sensible risk.

PEOPLE IN INDIANAPOLIS became familiar with a picture of Tom that appeared in several editions of their papers. The picture is cropped just below the knot of his tie and Tom is looking straight at the camera, as if it were his picture on a document. The lower right-hand corner of his white shirt is intersected by a small, almost rectangular patch of dark material: Nancy's shoulder; the portrait was a detail of a photograph taken at Christmas the year before of Tom and the family. The original version is attached by magnets to the side of the refrigerator in Nancy's kitchen. Along with a collection of other family pictures it forms a kind of shrine to the life they once had. The pictures hang on a side of the refrigerator that is partly obscured, and you would not see them unless you happened to step into the line of sight that reveals them. Someone examining them might come to the conclusion that Tom had only one expression for the camera. On any of the occasions on which some friend or relative or plain old witness thought to take his picture, he appears poised and thoughtful and slightly absent of an expression. He doesn't smile and he doesn't frown. There is not a trace in his appearance of anything you might consider prideful. If the picture is of a group of men, Tom is always to be found to one side. If there is a group of men and a trophy, Tom is not the one with his hand on it. He is capable-looking, and earnest and dependable, a minister perhaps, not dynamic possibly, but beloved by his congregation for his sympathy and attentiveness. What he was, actually, was a minister's grandson. His father, the minister's son, was a professor. Growing up, Tom always had to be quiet in the evenings so as not to disturb his father at work on his dissertation. There is no suggestion of malice or meanness to the man whose face appears on the front page of the paper. Perhaps he seems a bit aloof; maybe shy, maybe diffident. Perhaps it is only that he is trying not to draw attention to himself. In any case, it is difficult to look at the picture and absorb that the man it portrays is dead.

Nicholas and Christopher are now ten years old and fourteen. Neither looks much like his mother. They have their father's dark hair, and roughly the same broad shape to their faces. They have eager, searching eyes. Both boys give the impression by their manners of taking in quickly what is happening around them. A person who knew nothing about them might think them more solemn than the usual boy, perhaps more cautious and alert, as if something in their experience had led them to expect a shock to be revealed within an ordinary moment. They register the arrival of strangers. They seem at certain moments so grave and proper and sober as to be much older than they are, so it is sometimes surprising when they behave like children.

When the subject of death came up in school one day— this was nearly five years after the murder—Nicholas broke down. His class was reading a book with a plot that involved the death of the main character. The teacher had shown Nancy the two books she was considering—in each a character died—and asked her to select the one she thought Nicholas might have less difficulty with. Even so, while the class was discussing the book, the teacher noticed his distress and took him out into the hall to ask if he felt all right and he started to cry, and he cried again when Nancy came and picked him up, and he cried that night at home.

The patience most people have for someone else's grief is short-lived. The display of a measured grief is comforting. It implies order, and even benevolence (for being designed of sensible proportions) to processes of life that we don't understand well, can understand only if we have gone through them. Profound grief suggests mysteries at the heart of human existence that cannot be prepared for, which can come at any time, and into any life. Nancy is acquainted with widows whose mourning has been abbreviated by anxiety over how other people view them, and she occasionally feels pressure to have an uncomplicated relation to the loss of her husband. "Lots of women think you have to go on," she says. "They say this is not going to throw them. 'You have to get up and get a job,' they say, and the kids have their moment of grief and now it's over. This is what people want to hear, and if they hear it from you, they treat you better. You say, 'I'm fine,' and people are glad to hear it.

"I get so mad sometimes at people who say, 'Oh, she's doing fine,' because I'm not. I'm bleeding inside. I've had people say to me, 'Oh, you should be glad for what you had. And you never know what might have happened—Tom might have got cancer or your marriage fall apart or something else terrible have taken place.' I had another woman, the mother of a policeman, say, 'I just worry all the time about my son. Now at least that's over for you.' And it is not easy to hear this. For one thing, having had love and a good marriage for twelve years only makes you want more. For another, I never used to worry about Tom's safety, because his clients were not dangerous.

"I don't want to hear that I'm doing fine. If this is fine, I don't want any more of it."

What anger she expresses comes forth in the form of indignation over the senselessness of the murder. "He should never have died," she says. "Not that kind of person, not that kind of father. It shouldn't have happened. Not through the prison system, not through the probation system. Somebody should have prevented it. But it does harm only to me to allow all these 'if only's'; it would only hurt me. It wouldn't hurt Jackson; he's gone and I couldn't have touched him anyway.

"In this whole big world, though, that these two people had to come together at five after eight on that morning. There are so many other possibilities, why was he different on that morning than he was on Sunday morning? He wasn't killing anyone then. Why did they have to come together in that spot, in that deserted place, with all those deserted souls? It has always seemed that way to me. Whenever I've been to the house I haven't ever seen anyone else. I don't know if people are staring at me from behind their curtains, but there's never anyone on the street. It always seems a lonely and forlorn place.

"Jackson could have needed something from the store and got in his truck and gone off and Tom arrived and left a note. Or Tom could have gone somewhere else first and stopped off there and missed him. So that's when I pray for peace—because there are no answers for that—so I don't go into turmoil over all the things I have no answers for."

When Nancy is running through her list of anxieties, she will sometimes pause to entertain the one in which she worries about the effect the murder of their father will have on the boys as they grow. "Tom was always doing case studies of families," she says, "trying to figure out what happened, and so often there would be stories where everything once seemed fine in a family and then some tragedy like this took place and the boys turned hostile or violent, and got into trouble, and I worry so much that this will happen to them."

An unsettling aspect of raising Nicholas and Christopher is that Nancy never feels she can be sure whether a piece of problematic behavior is a matter of their characters and personalities, or their age, or has happened only because their father is dead.

At night, sitting on their beds and talking to them in the darkness, she would answer a question they had by telling them that the man who murdered their father was sick and living in a state that made it seem almost as if he were an animal. She would tell them God had not wanted their father murdered. She had come to think of Mike Jackson as evil, as sin standing in front of Tom, and as if evil had taken him from the world, but she kept this to herself. She studied Jackson's photograph on the wanted poster and absorbed that wild stare. She felt haunted by the thought that those were the last eyes Tom looked into. She knows that whatever she tells Nicholas and Christopher about Mike Jackson, they still wonder how he could have done what he did. "I know he made the world a more fearful, violent place for them in a way it might not have been."

It is difficult for Nancy to bear knowing very much about Mike Jackson. If there is an explanation for him, if what he did makes sense when separated from any point of view but his own, then it is possible for something malevolent to happen to her and Nicholas and Christopher again. Part of recovering involves assessing one's safety. It is easier to view him as an aberration. If he is an act of God, that is one thing. If he is a man who struggled to contain impulses that more often than not overpowered him, and that no one seemed able to help him understand, then he is different from most of the rest of us only in the severity of his disorder, not in its content.

Mike inhabits the darker quarters of the boys' imaginations. He is a demon, with a territory. And it does not ask much of the imagination to believe that a demon within us might also exist somewhere in the world. Mike not only occupied his place in the world, but where it was happened to be not far from the normal daylight occurrences of their lives. Tom had breakfast with Nicholas and Christopher and Nancy, drove off from their home, and twenty minutes later met a man, not by chance, a man who was part of the routine of his working life, who turned out to be a maniac capable of shooting him in the head with a shotgun until he was more than sure he was dead. If such a man existed, there could be others.

AFTER A FEW YEARS Christopher's need to talk every night began to trail off. He began not to want to hear anything at night about what happened to his father, and he still doesn't. Evenings in which his father has been talked about sometimes end with Christopher's wanting to see a picture of him before going to bed. And then trouble getting to sleep. At the end of certain days when his father had been a presence, he sometimes needed to have his room searched. Nevertheless, his defenses sometimes fall to curiosity, or to the desire to know more, to bring more of what happened into the light, and then there is a period of recovery. Nicholas still occasionally talks to his mother about his father before going to sleep, and when Christopher hears him through the wall, he yells out to him to shut up. If Nancy says about Jackson, "He's dead, he can't hurt us anymore," Christopher will reply, "How can you say that to me just when I'm going to bed!"

No one called with an offer to handle her money. A contractor who repaired the roof of her house presented himself for a position having nothing to do with his profession. A man who worked for the post office sent a letter through her church, which worried her because she thought he might find her address. A man called within two weeks of the murder saying he saw her picture in the paper. Another called a few months later, saying that now that she was a widow maybe he could keep her company. Salesmen call in the course of their work and ask for her husband, and she knows not to let on she's a widow, but recently she slipped with an aluminum siding salesman she called for an estimate. He showed up half an hour early for his appointment and asked if he could come in. He asked if he could sit down, then asked if he could smoke a cigar. He told her he had lost his wife and then he asked if she'd like to have dinner with him after he got back from Las Vegas. She bought vinyl siding.

The calls she occasionally gets from men she doesn't know make her nervous, but she fields them politely and doesn't let on what she's feeling for fear of bringing down more trouble on herself.

OVER THE YEARS Jackson began to figure more often in dreams the boys had. Nicholas once dreamed he was torturing Jackson, burning holes with a cigarette in the skin of his arm to the bone. Christopher dreamed Jackson followed him in a car. In another dream, Jackson was tied to a wall and Christopher and a companion had a collection of knives they could throw at him. They shaved his head. Recently, Christopher dreamed he saw the image of Jackson everywhere he turned. There seemed to be about sixty of him. They were at school and they were at home, and they would surround him and hiss and bare their teeth whenever he approached. He told Nancy about the dream in the morning and she felt that it represented a movement forward— at least the figures of Jackson had intended only to scare him, not kill him.

During the first few years of being a widow, Nancy did not know much about the lives of any other widows. Whatever groups she thought of taking part in met in the evenings, and she did not want to leave Christopher and Nicholas to attend. During the second year after Tom was killed Nancy began meeting for lunch with a friend whose husband had died. They would try to get together every six weeks. Gradually they invited other women until over the years the occasion grew to involve several, none of whose circumstances much resembled any other's. One woman's husband was murdered in the city late at night and found in a parking lot. Another woman lost hers in a construction accident. One husband had a heart attack. Another stopped at a hotel to make a phone call and died from burns he received in a fire that started when a plane crashed into the hotel. One woman and her husband were driving back from leaving their daughter at college in the East when a tire fell off a truck and came through their windshield with such force that it broke her husband's neck. A man whose wife died of cancer two weeks after delivering their child occasionally attends. Nancy has been a widow longer than anyone else in the group. She mostly listens. She feels that people tell her things and that there must be some reason for it, so it must be important to listen.

The women exchange strategies for dealing with social security. They talk about how much time passed before it felt right to wear makeup again. Sometimes they talk about dating. One woman's wedding was called off at the church because the groom didn't show. They talk about their children and their sense of loss and whether they should have their mothers live with them to help with the family while they work. They talk about their sons having difficulty with other men coming into the house. They worry mainly about their children and how they will survive. Some women simply put on a smile and don't seem to be paying any attention at all to their feelings. One woman said, "I just want to stay in the darkness."

IN THE SPRING of 1991, the husband of a woman Nancy knows was shot and killed in Indianapolis. When Nicholas and Christopher heard the news they began sleeping in the same room.

Nancy still occasionally wakes early on Monday mornings and looks at the clock and thinks, Was he dead yet? She feels that each day will bring her at least one reminder that her husband is dead. Every time one of the boys has a success in school or wins an award for sports, he says that he wishes his father were there to share it with him, or he asks Nancy if she thinks it is possible that his father can see him.

She lies awake sometimes at night and wonders if Mike Jackson would have killed anyone who came to his door that morning. She tries to imagine him during that last night. Did he sleep? Spend the whole night staring at the wall? Did he walk out into the darkness and gaze up at the sky? It strikes her as almost inexplicably strange that before killing her husband he was engaged in something as ordinary as pounding a dent on his truck. How did he move in his mind from carrying out a chore to performing an execution?

Until recently a brother of hers lived down the street and was around to start the lawn tractor when the spark wouldn't catch, or lift heavy things, or repair the gas grill when she couldn't get it to ignite, but he and his wife bought a bigger house half an hour away, so she is forced now to do more on her own. She sometimes finds herself crying while trying to repair an electrical switch, or a toaster that won't do what it's supposed to, and thinking, I never wanted to know how to do this. We meant to raise our children together and give them a family.

She keeps the front door locked during the day. On the door itself is a small brass plaque inscribed "Mr. and Mrs. Thomas E. Gahl."

When Nicholas and Christopher miss their father, she tries to think of funny things he did to make them feel better. She reminds Nicholas that his father chased him upstairs at night when it was time for his bath and tickled him if he caught him. For a while Nicholas remembered the experience clearly. Now he says, "I *think* that's what he did."

The first thing that comes to Christopher's mind when he remembers doing things with his father is an image of playing baseball with him. The memories that Nicholas recalls have more to do with his father instructing him in the use of the tools in his shop in the garage. This bothers Christopher. He wonders whether it was wrong for him to have spent less time with his father as he got older. Nicholas sometimes resents Christopher's having had a longer life with their father. Christopher sometimes resents the time that his father and Nicholas spent together while Christopher was off on his bike. When he leaves the house in the morning, in addition to telling Nancy that he loves her, Christopher obsessively says he is sorry for all the things he has done wrong. A year or so before Tom died, he said to Nancy, "If anything ever happens to me, will you be sure to tell the boys how much I love them," and she is grateful she has that to pass along.

Nancy thinks that she might not renew her subscription to the magazine *Bereavement*. If that were her decision it would be a step forward, she feels. She still frequently summons her husband to her mind, still opens the door of his closet and looks at his clothes, still occasionally takes down from the attic the clothes he was wearing when he was shot. The clothes she wore that day she has never put on again; they hang in her closet. When the anniversary of the murder arrives, she visits the house where Mike Jackson lived. On the fourth anniversary she was unable to find it. Some months later she went with a friend of the family who told her he knew where it was. It happened to be a night when the boys were at a baseball game. It turned out that her friend was mistaken in his directions and they wandered for a while in the city, stopping at gas stations to ask where they were. Nancy grew concerned about getting home in time for the boys' return. She and the friend came around a corner and the house appeared suddenly in front of them. Nancy sat in the car staring at the place where her husband lay. Tears came to her eyes. She said, "Oh, damn." Then, "Honey, why'd he have to hurt you so bad?"

About four years after the murder, Nancy gave some of Tom's clothes to an assistant pastor of her church, who was moving to Kansas. "Tom was about five eleven," she says, "big in the shoulders and with big legs, and the assistant pastor was the same build, so he could wear them, and he was going far enough away that we wouldn't be shocked by seeing them on someone else. I kept some suits and things that the boys might want someday, and I'm not ready to get rid of them yet anyway. Whenever I read about grieving, they say that you shouldn't do anything at least for a year

—don't sell your house, don't give things away—because it takes that long to get back to the point where you can make decisions you can trust. I know that I am way past the point of a year, but I still don't feel ready. I read somewhere about one widow who gave away her husband's clothes and then really wanted them. Luckily she found a robe he had worn and that she could put on and feel as if his arms were around her."

A friend found a videotape with Tom in it coaching a baseball game. You could hear his voice and see the way he carried himself when he ran, and because of watching that the boys asked to see the collection of news reports their mother compiled. Nancy has a videotape player in her car. When she and the boys take long trips she brings along tapes to keep them occupied. Recently she and Nicholas and Christopher were driving to St. Louis. Nicholas and Christopher watched the tape, saw again the picture of their father covered by a sheet, saw the bloodstain by his head, and heard people talking about him, and they cried, and Nancy cried watching them as she drove down the highway.

On the Father's Day five years after the murder Nancy took the boys to visit her father and his wife. That night, in his grandfather's house, Christopher dreamed he got up in the morning and put his pajamas under his pillow, as he usually does, then turned and saw Jackson in the window. Christopher tried to run, but Jackson shot him from behind. Christopher told Nancy he knew in the dream he was hit, but was not dead. A while later, Nancy realized that what happened to Christopher with Jackson in the dream was exactly what had happened to her husband.

The boys find themselves sometimes on the lawn on a

summer's night, staring up through the trees at the sky and stars above them. Their father's body has now lain in the cemetery for five years. The sky is where they look for him. His death has left them alone in a way they never expected to be. Along with their mother they wonder what more is to be asked of them. A step at a time they have been climbing from the hole dug for them by somebody else.

AUTHOR'S NOTE

THIS BOOK BEGAN as a Profile for *The New Yorker* of the tracker JR Buchanan. The idea was given to me by Ian Frazier.

I also feel indebted to the following people, whose names do not appear in the text:

At *The New Yorker*: Nancy Boensch, Judy Callender, Rich Cohen, Grace Darby, Bruce Diones, Robert Gottlieb, Eleanor Gould, Beverley Hamilton, Martha Kaplan, Nicholas Parker, and Pearl Powell.

Deborah Garrison, Adam Gopnik, and Charles McGrath, who read early versions of the manuscript, and especially to Hal Espen and C. Patrick Crow for the time and attention they devoted to shaping the version of this book that appeared in the magazine.

At Alfred A. Knopf: Paul Bogaards, Nina Bourne, Jane Friedman, Janice Goldklang, Katherine Hourigan, Barbara Jones-Diggs, Ann Kraybill, Nicholas Latimer, William Loverd, and A. S. Mehta.

I would also particularly like to thank Andrew Wylie and Sarah Chalfant, Ann Close, Reynolds Price, and Joseph Fox.

What I owe William Maxwell I cannot sufficiently express.

A NOTE ON THE TYPE

This book was set on the Linotype in Granjon, a type named in compliment to Robert Granjon, a type cutter and printer active, in Antwerp, Lyons, Rome, and Paris, from 1523 to 1590. Granjon, the boldest and most original designer of his time, was one of the first to practice the trade of type founder apart from that of printer.

Linotype Granjon was designed by George W. Jones, who based his drawings on a face used by Claude Garamond (c. 1480–1561) in his beautiful French books. Granjon more closely resembles Garamond's own type than does any of the various modern faces that bear his name.

Composed by PennSet, Inc.,
Bloomsburg, Pennsylvania

Printed and bound by The Haddon Craftsmen,
Scranton, Pennsylvania

Designed by Mia Vander Els

2/93